FAITH AT
HOME

FAITH AT HOME

A Handbook for Cautiously Christian Parents

WENDY CLAIRE BARRIE

Morehouse Publishing
NEW YORK

Unless otherwise noted, the Scripture quotations contained herein are from the New Revised Standard Version Bible, copyright © 1989 by the Division of Christian Education of the National Council of Churches of Christ in the U.S.A. Used by permission. All rights reserved.

Scripture taken from the Common English Bible®, CEB® Copyright © 2010, 2011 by Common English Bible.™ Used by permission. All rights reserved worldwide. The "CEB" and "Common English Bible" trademarks are registered in the United States Patent and Trademark Office by Common English Bible. Use of either trademark requires the permission of Common English Bible.

Stories of many of the saints within these pages (Martin Luther King, Jr., Martin of Tours, Mary Magdalene, St. Francis of Assisi, and Nicholas of Myra) written by Wendy Claire Barrie were previously published online in *Lesson Plans that Work* © 2014 The Domestic & Foreign Missionary Society of the Protestant Episcopal Church of the United States of America. Used with permission.

"Flowing Stream" from *Heart* ©2016 Brook Packard / Sleepytime Club. Used with permission.

Morehouse Publishing, 19 East 34th Street, New York, NY 10016

Morehouse Publishing is an imprint of Church Publishing Incorporated.
www.churchpublishing.org

Cover design by Laurie Klein Westhafer, Bounce Design
Typeset by Beth Oberholtzer

Library of Congress Cataloging-in-Publication Data
Names: Barrie, Wendy Claire, author.
Title: Faith at home : a handbook for cautiously Christian parents / Wendy
    Claire Barrie.
Description: New York : Morehouse Publishing, 2016. | Includes
    bibliographical references.
Identifiers: LCCN 2016026038 | ISBN 9780819232762 (pbk.) | ISBN
    9780819232779 (ebook)
Subjects: LCSH: Christian education—Home training. | Christian education of
    children. | Families—Religious life.
Classification: LCC BV1590 .B37 2016 | DDC 248.8/45—dc23 LC record available
    at https://lccn.loc.gov/2016026038

Printed in the United States of America

For my mother, Deborah,
for my son, Peter,
and for my husband, Phil,
who have strengthened and enriched beyond
measure my faith at home and in the world.

Contents

Introduction

You have picked up this book, or some well-meaning person has given it to you, because you are interested in passing on your Christian faith to your kids, or you would like to pass on a different understanding of the Christian faith than the one you grew up with, or because you are new to being a Christian and you've noticed it's counter-cultural, revolutionary, and not quite what mainstream culture would have us believe. Come on in, the water's fine!

Some years ago I remember being both surprised and indignant when a coworker at the Metropolitan Museum of Art described me as "religious." It seemed vaguely insulting and possibly untrue, even though I was employed part-time as the Sunday school director at a nearby Episcopal church and had previously taught for seven years at an Episcopal school. I had grown up in a more-than-nominally Christian household going to church every week, but I didn't feel *religious*. I just felt comfortable talking about, wondering about, and arguing about matters of faith.

Not long after that, I read a book that changed my life: *Offering the Gospel to Children*, by Gretchen Wolff Pritchard. Suddenly I found a whole new vocabulary for talking about matters of faith with parents and children, clergy, and church decision makers. I also found a calling, colleagues who supported and challenged me, and families who invited me to walk alongside them. In 2003 my son Peter was born, and having worked with children and youth my entire adult life (with the exception of that short tenure at the Met), I soon repented of many things I both said to parents and thought about parents before I became a parent myself. There is one rule I stick to, and as you read this book I offer it to you: Do what works. It's that simple. Try what appeals to you. If it works, keep doing it. If it doesn't, try something else. There are things that are worth trying more than once, because not everything works right away. There are things worth trying again later, because some things work after you wait a while. Trust your instincts, though. Practicing faith at home takes just that: practice.

Here's something else to keep in mind: faith at home, at church, and out in the world is best thought of as a journey. It's not something we finally get right, or even finish. Rarely is it something we do alone. We are in this together and with God.

It may help you to consider that the word "believe" comes from the German word for love, *liebe.* Our creed begins with the words "I believe." Creed comes from the Latin *credo,* which has the same root as heart. "Believe" is used so differently today, but what might it do for us if what we believe was about what we give our hearts to instead of what we think?[1] For its first five hundred years, Christianity was understood "primarily as spiritual practices that offered a meaningful way of life in this world," Diana Butler Bass reminds us. They called themselves followers of the Way, understanding that it was how they lived and not what they thought or believed that identified them as Christians.[2]

So let's start there: trying to follow the teachings of Jesus and the pattern of his life, and talking with our kids about how and why we do it as we go. While none of this is easy, it should never be boring. The presiding bishop of the Episcopal Church, Michael Curry, calls us "Crazy Christians."

> Crazy enough to love like Jesus, to give like Jesus, to forgive like Jesus, to do justice, love mercy, walk humbly with God—like Jesus. Crazy enough to dare to change the world from the nightmare it often is into something close to the dream that God dreams for it.[3]

We have our work cut out for us, and it's the work of a lifetime.

I wrote this book to share with you my journey of faith as a parent with my own child, and as someone who has worked with children, youth, and families in Episcopal churches for a long time now. I certainly don't have all the answers, but I am happy to offer my questions and share some of what I have found along the Way.

The poet Christian Wiman wrote, "So perhaps one doesn't teach children about God so much as help them grow into what they already know, and perhaps 'know' is precisely the wrong verb."[4] In Matthew 24:17, Jesus annoyed his disciples who were shooing away parents bringing their children to him:

He called a child, whom he put among them, and said, "Truly I tell you, unless you change and become like children, you will never enter the kingdom of heaven."

I wonder if Jesus meant that to know, love, and serve God requires imagination and heart, openness, and curiosity. There is much we can learn from our children.

CHAPTER 1

Talking about God

The Lord said, "Go out and stand at the mountain before the Lord. The Lord is passing by." A very strong wind tore through the mountains and broke apart the stones before the Lord. But the Lord wasn't in the wind. After the wind, there was an earthquake. But the Lord wasn't in the earthquake. After the earthquake, there was a fire. But the Lord wasn't in the fire. After the fire, there was a sound. Thin. Quiet. When Elijah heard it, he wrapped his face in his coat. He went out and stood at the cave's entrance. A voice came to him and said, "Why are you here, Elijah?" 1 Kings 19:11–13 (CEB)

"Oh, sure," you're probably thinking, "people talked about God and with God all the time in those days, and everyone agreed on what God is like. Nobody doubted or struggled with their faith. It's so different from today and my experience." Stay with me here.

The passage from the first book of Kings that begins this chapter has always fascinated me. Here's the backstory: The prophet Elijah has called on God's power and witnessed more than his share of dramatic miracles—enough food in famine, fire from heaven, answered prayer in the form of drought-ending rain, raising a child from the dead. At this point in the story, though, Elijah has given up on God. That it could happen to him shows that it can happen to anyone. He runs for his life and hides in a cave, defeated and depressed. What next? God comes to Elijah, not in the stone-breaking wind, not in the earthquake, not in the fire. God comes to Elijah in silence, in what the King James Version calls "the still small voice"[1] of God. Just when we, in our disheartened disbelief, think we have God all figured out, God is in what we do not expect. As surprising as it may seem, as one mainline denomination puts it, "God is still speaking."[2]

Let's talk about God, or say—at least—that we want to, if not in public or with our friends, then at home with our kids. Many of us, even those who count ourselves believers, do not talk about God. It's easier and more comfortable and a lot less dangerous that way. However, let's take the risk. Let's agree that we can talk about God without trying to prove the existence of God. Doubts are welcome here. Let's also name that talking about God in this day and age is complicated by the fact that many of us don't agree on who or what

God is. What we are trying to articulate for our children may be drastically different from the understanding of God that we grew up with. Our thoughts and beliefs may not be what are commonly accepted in popular culture, or even in our extended families.

Where do we start? It's easy to understand why we personify God, why we make God like us, only bigger, stronger, more powerful. There are consequences, however, to trying to make God more relatable. American teenagers overwhelmingly view God as "a combination Divine Butler and Cosmic Therapist" whose job is "to solve our problems and make people feel good," according to Christian Smith, the principal investigator of the National Study of Youth and Religion.[3] The research tells us this is not simply a matter of misunderstanding. This is the God that we, their parents and their churches, have given them. We have failed to introduce them to the God of invitation and imagination, the God of the burning bush and the still small voice, the God of living water and rushing wind, in whom "we live and move and have our being."[4]

Talking the Talk

The first problem Smith and his collaborator Melinda Denton identify is that most U.S. teenagers are *"incredibly inarticulate* about their faith, their religious beliefs and practices, and its meaning or place in their lives."[5] Why? "Religious language is like any other language; to learn how to speak it, one first needs to listen to native speakers using it a lot, and then one needs plenty of practice speaking it oneself."[6] In other words, our kids first need to hear us talk about God, what we believe, and why it matters.

So *how* do we talk about God? The theologian Elizabeth Johnson offers three ground rules from early Christian thought:

1. God is a mystery.
2. No name or image of God should be taken literally.
3. There are many and varied expressions of God.[7]

Above all, Johnson encourages us to speak of "the living God," not "this invisible, greatly powerful grand old man in the sky."[8] God as super-parent who must be obeyed is especially unattractive to young people, she points out, who may be rebelling against parents in general.[9] (Imagine that.) The living God, an image found throughout the Bible, is creative, active, present, and new. The living God is the one I *want* to talk about, the one I love, the one who is Love.

Metaphor and Mystery

What is God like? *Images of God for Young Children* by Marie-Hélène Delval chooses forty among the hundreds of biblical images in child-friendly (though frequently male-gendered) language and bright, evocative illustrations. Two perennial picture book favorites are Rabbi Sandy Eisenberg Sasso's *In God's Name*, perfect for kids in preschool and early elementary school, and *Old Turtle* by Douglas Wood, excellent for older elementary ages. In these books, God is revealed in ways that are familiar and surprising, personal and wondrous.

We get stuck when we divide up the world and everything else into what we know and what we believe, the rational and the miraculous, the ordinary and the holy. Christians should know better: Jesus embodies both. As pastor Rob Bell puts it, "When we talk about Jesus being divine and human, what we are saying is that Jesus, in a unique, singular and historic way, shows us what God is like."[10] If you have trouble talking about God, try talking about Jesus. We've had some success with that.

One afternoon at home when Peter was seven, the phone rang and Peter came running upstairs while I was chatting with the caller. He was breathless and impatient, hopping up and down from foot to foot. When I hung up, he asked with great excitement, "Mommy, was that Jesus?!" Puzzled, I told him no, it was a priest calling from another church. What made him think that? He was crestfallen, "The caller ID said 'Good Shepherd.'" That image of Jesus so real to Peter was one he recognized from both Sunday school and the Bible: the Good Shepherd who calls us each by name, whose voice we know and follow, who lays down his life for the sheep.

Let's talk about God in metaphor and mystery, in simple concrete ways: as a mother hen, a friend, a gardener, as artist and builder, as light and rock. Let's talk about what we imagine when we say "God." Words will fail us here. That's a *good* thing. It is where we start, but not where we end up. The living God is calling us, moving us forward, inviting us to help bring heaven to earth, "reclaiming the planet an inch at a time" as Sister Joan Chittister says, "until the Garden of Eden grows green again."

CHAPTER 2

Talking with God

have never prayed more often or more simply than when I was pregnant. My constant prayer before Peter was born was "Please." Afterward, for nearly as many months, my prayer was "Thank you." It was all I could manage, and all that felt necessary. I don't know how prayer works. I don't believe that prayer changes outcome, but that has never kept me from praying. "The prayer does not change God, but it changes the one who prays."[1] Prayer understands the importance of naming that which is too hard, too awful, too wonderful, and giving it over to the power which is beyond us.

What is prayer? Anne Lamott in her terrific book *Help, Thanks, Wow: The Three Essential Prayers* defines prayer as "communication from one's heart to God."[2] Communication is key here. Prayer is conversation. It's not just us, talking or asking. We are also deeply listening with our hearts. Sometimes it's helpful to talk about what prayer is not. Prayer is not a Christmas list, and God is not Santa Claus. Prayer is not about what we want or even what we wish for, although it might be about what we really need, or what we most deeply hope for. Prayer does not assume or expect answers. That's the hardest part. Why, then, do we pray? Prayer brings us close to God. When we pray for someone in need, we are lifting them to God's presence. When we pray for our own needs, we are giving them over to God.

How do we pray? When do we pray? The Book of Common Prayer (which is full of great stuff—you should definitely get one) says that prayer is "responding to God, by thought and by deeds, with or without words."[3] That's from the Catechism, an outline of the faith found at the back of the Book of Common Prayer that is a basic summary of what is broadly taught in Episcopal churches. What a tremendously freeing description: responding, by thought and by deeds, with or without words. This means prayer can be just about anything, any time, anywhere. We don't have to be in church or around the table or kneeling beside our beds. We don't even have to be still. We don't need a book or a script or words at all. Prayer is about intention: Set aside the time, make a space for God and for sharing what is on your heart or mind. You don't even have to call it prayer. You can call it family time or quiet time, and then together reflect on how it was also time spent with God.

Silence

Prayer can be silence, even for children. Ring a bell or strike a chime and keep silence sitting together, feet on the floor or seated on a cushion until the sound fades away. Gradually stretch the time of keeping silence to three minutes, five minutes, ten minutes. That's when it gets really interesting. Meditation and mindfulness techniques are great for all ages. They help us become more attuned to the presence of God, letting stillness and silence heighten our awareness, diminishing the sounds of the noisy world and the distractions of our own thoughts, which separate us from our true selves. This is time and space apart.

Music

Music can be prayer. According to St. Augustine (354–430 CE), to sing is to pray twice! What songs or pieces of music bring you close to God? Ask the same question of your teenager on a regular basis because they will have new responses each time. You could make a mix of tunes for family listening with closeness to God in mind. It could be Bach, jazz, reggae, or rap. Does this mean going to a concert can be prayerful? Absolutely. So can going to church, even if one goes "just for the music," which is sometimes the reason my son, who sings in the choir, gives. We have been known to sing at bedtime. It can be a hymn, a lullaby, or Bob Dylan's "Forever Young"—all gentle tunes to calm the busy day.

Praying with Our Bodies

Making the sign of the cross (by touching the forehead, sternum, left shoulder, right shoulder and sternum again) is a body prayer, which I have long understood as a way of drawing God into us. Yoga and tai chi are ways of praying with the body. Although they come from other religious traditions, they can be equally prayerful for Christians. I asked a friend whether she saw a connection between her son's karate practice (rigorous, several days a week) and prayer. When she asked him, Harry (age eleven) immediately responded, "I can't explain it, but it connects me to God somehow."

Our bodies are in touch with the holy in ways words cannot explain. Dance can be embodied prayer. Please search online for Stephen Colbert dancing to "King of Glory, King of Peace" and know that laughter, too, can be a way of praying.

Walking and hiking can be ways to pray. When you walk, take care to notice the presence of God, which will be obvious in nature. Waterfalls, streams, the ocean, trees, meadows and mountains, the sunset, and the starry sky all tell us of the glory of God. As you walk, your kids might collect acorns, colored leaves, or interesting stones to set in a shallow bowl in the center of your table, or wildflowers to put in a jam jar. Preschoolers can be given an egg carton with a different color painted in each recess and asked to find something from God's creation to place in it. Older kids can take photos (with a smart phone?) of where they find God in nature, or in the neighborhood. On a city or suburban walk, notice which people (the dog walkers, the grocery baggers) or places (the car wash and all who drive through it, the diner and those who prepare the food we enjoy) can be included in your prayers. Notice, too, where prayers are being answered: The soup kitchen? The hospital? The art museum?

Labyrinths

Walking a labyrinth is a wonderful way for adults and kids to pray. Labyrinths are different from mazes: there is only one way in and one way out, so you can't get lost. It's a journey to the center and out again, providing a clear path and a walking rhythm that promotes inner calm. Find out if there is a labyrinth near you. Churches and cathedrals are obvious locations, but they turn up in unexpected places such as children's hospitals, too. There is a labyrinth at the tip of Manhattan in Battery Park, created to commemorate the first anniversary of the World Trade Center tragedy.

If you are feeling adventurous you can draw one with sidewalk chalk or mark one on a lawn with stones or pool noodles. Last summer at a medieval-themed summer camp we laid out a labyrinth on the auditorium floor with masking tape, dimmed the lights, put on a CD of Gregorian chant and sent mixed-age groups of six- to eighteen-year-olds through, with about thirty seconds between each participant. The teenagers were shocked by how quiet and reverent the young ones were, and how many times they wanted to walk through slowly and in silence. Afterward, when I asked them what they noticed about the experience, an eight-year-old told me she came close to God there.

Coloring and Doodling

Making art, coloring a mandala, even doodling can be prayer. Set up an art corner, or if you live in a small space make an art box and fill it with heavy white paper, scraps of ribbon, old greeting cards, colored pencils, marking pens, glue sticks, a pair of scissors. My favorite art activity is to make collages—small ones, about the size of a postcard— just right for a prayer card, a get-well card, or a thank you card to give away. There are amazing coloring books available now that are perfect for praying: intricate patterns, nature designs, and symbols of faith. Sybil MacBeth found herself unable to concentrate, short of words, and needing to pray. She took a pad of paper and a basket of markers out to the porch, drew a leaf shape and wrote her friend's name inside it. Soon her page was covered with shapes and names, colors and designs. Sybil had discovered prayer through doodling and subsequently wrote a book about how to do it: *Praying in Color.* When I introduced this form to a group of middle school choristers, twelve-year-old Eli turned to a friend and said with surprise, "I never knew praying could be so much fun!"

Praying with Words

Some people are completely comfortable praying aloud extemporaneously, finding in the moment the just-right words that are needed for a given situation. I am not one of those people. Praying aloud off the top of my head or even from my heart has always seemed a little weird to me. I can pray without words or silently while standing at the kitchen sink or under the shower or at the beach (there is something about water that puts me in mind of prayer), but I find myself profoundly grateful for other writers when it comes time for me to pray in public. This, as you might imagine, has been an occupational hazard. So I write prayers to read aloud on special occasions, and widely borrow them from others. I don't want to discourage you from praying off the cuff; I only mean to say that if it doesn't come easily, you are not alone.

The Lord's Prayer

When the disciples asked Jesus how to pray, he gave them one we still use, the Lord's Prayer. It's a very good one to learn because it can be used for any occasion:

Our Father, who art in heaven, hallowed be thy name. Thy kingdom come, thy will be done on earth as it is in heaven. Give us this day our daily bread. And forgive us our trespasses as we forgive those who trespass against us. Lead us not into temptation but deliver us from evil. For thine is the kingdom, the power and the glory forever. Amen.

What does the Lord's Prayer mean? We pray to God, parent of us all, who knows us better and loves us more than anyone else. God's name is holy. Bringing God's kingdom to earth makes the whole world holy, too, as God means for it to be: a place of peace and harmony and justice. We ask for what we need. We tell God we are sorry when we "trespass" or cross the line and we share the forgiveness God gives us with others. Keep us from the wrong path, protect us from harm. Everything comes from God, and in thanks for all we have been given we return praise to God. There is a wonderful rhythm in this, a pattern for our prayer life: giving God praise, dedicating ourselves to God's good work, petitioning God for what we and others most need, and confessing our wrongdoings are all embedded in this one prayer.

Grace at Meals

If you are new to praying with your kids, start where it feels most comfortable. Table graces might be familiar from holiday gatherings, preschool snack time, or summer camp. Choose a book, have your kids copy some onto index cards, and let each person take turns choosing one to read aloud. Sung graces are great for little ones. If you sing the Doxology in church, start with that:

Praise God from whom all blessings flow, praise God all creatures here below, Praise God above ye heavenly host, Praise Father, Son and Holy Ghost.

The first grace Peter learned is sung to the tune of "Frere Jacques":

God our father, God our mother, we thank you, we thank you, for this food before us, for this food before us. Amen, amen.

Friends and family are a great resource for collecting graces and blessings from other cultures and religious traditions, which can be a great way "in" to this universal and timeless tradition.

The Quakers have a very simple said grace:

Us and this, God bless.

Their most common form of grace, however, is everyone holding hands around the table in silence. It's easy to add the invitation to each person to name something for which they are thankful. Cultivating a practice of gratitude, a habit of noticing and naming what we are thankful for is of profound benefit to our physical, spiritual, and emotional health.[4] You could keep a thankfulness journal that each family member contributes to throughout the year, or use the month of November to ask each person to write their thanksgivings on leaves of colored paper to fill a jar or a window. Peter noticed and remarked on a significant decrease in complaints when our household became more intentionally grateful.

Bedtime

Bedtime prayers are a beloved ritual in many homes, easing the transition from day into night and giving child and parent a chance to reflect together on past events and present needs. Young children may want to name those they love and be reminded of those who love them. When Peter was tiny, I sang a version of this very old spiritual to him at bedtime—even naptime—adding names that included family and eventually classmates, teachers and neighbors:

Peter, Jesus loves you, Peter, Mommy loves you, and love, love, love comes trickling down.

Older children may take the opportunity to pray for their own needs and those of others. To say what we have done wrong or left undone at the end of the day and ask God's forgiveness is an act of confession and one that often leads to a more peaceful rest.

One form of prayer that lends itself well to the close of day is the *Examen*, a reflective practice developed by the fifteenth century saint, Ignatius of Loyola. It can be done with the whole family, with a parent and child, or by a teen in private, especially if you model it as a family practice first. The *Examen* begins with an invitation to notice God's presence. You could light a candle. Next, take turns recalling something that made you grateful today. Then name your sorrows and your joys or lows and highs from the day—just a few. Wonder together where you found God in them. Think ahead to tomorrow. What are you looking forward to? Ask God to be present in that, too. Conclude with the Lord's Prayer or any words of your own to bring these thoughts together. That's it, the *Examen* at its simplest.

Compline is the ancient service of night prayers dating to at least the sixth century, the last of the monastic "hours" traditionally said or sung just before bed. For two years Peter and I said Compline together sitting at the foot of his bed almost every night; we have said Compline together over the phone when I am traveling. This is a lovely way to end the evening. The service is brief and meaningful. It's easier for readers, but not difficult for non-readers to learn the responses. Anyone can lead the service, which is found on page 127 of the Book of Common Prayer.

For the first year of middle school, the bedtime prayer that most resonated with Peter was the "Prayer for Anxiety," found in *Call on Me: A Prayer Book for Young People* by my good friends Jenifer Gamber and Sharon Pearson:

Calm me.
Release everything that's making me anxious, especially

(name whatever is pressing in upon you).

Fill every cell of my body with your presence.
Help me feel your love everywhere:
 in my body, in my brain and in my soul.
Hold me in your arms
 so I can let this tension go.
Your love is stronger than anything.[5]

We tweaked it slightly it to include that which brought him comfort.

Now we most often say together the prayer that ends Compline, attributed to St. Augustine of Hippo:

Keep watch, dear Lord, with those who work or watch or weep this night, and give your angels charge over those who sleep. Tend the sick, Lord Christ, give rest to the weary, bless the dying, soothe the suffering, shield the joyous, and all for your love's sake. Amen.[6]

As I have since he was born, I make the sign of the cross on his forehead with my thumb and whisper words of blessing.

A New Zealand Prayer Book has a particularly good night prayer that begins:

Lord, it is night. The night is for stillness. Let us be still in the presence of God. It is night after a long day. What has been done has been done; what has not been done has not been done; let it be.[7]

Psalms

In times of great need, my prayer has long been the Twenty-Third Psalm:

The Lord is my shepherd, I shall not be in want . . .

I know it by heart and it seems that I always have, so that even when I am wordless the words come to me, reminding me of God's comfort, goodness, and mercy. The Psalms are a great reminder that there is a prayer for every occasion. It is never *not* a good time to pray. People in really bad moods wrote many of the psalms. It is important to remember that these psalms tell us less about God than they do about what it is to be human, and they also remind us that God is big enough to hold us in all our emotions: anger, despair, grief, sorrow, loneliness, longing, awe, joy, love.

Amen

There will be times when prayer is not nearly enough, and when unanswered prayer feels like abandonment or the absence of God entirely. That will take another chapter (and a lifetime) to delve into—please see chapter 7: Finding God in Difficult Times.

Christians and Jews end prayers with a declarative, amen, which in Hebrew means "firm." It is nearly the same for Muslims, who use the related Arabic word "amin." Think of it as a strong YES. Let it be so.

Pray in whatever way works for you and your family, pray when you can, and especially when you can't do anything else because this is something we can *do*: it is a way of coming close to God, wherever we are physically or emotionally. Pray for what you need, what your loved ones need, what the world needs. Give thanks, give praise, give your heart. And let the people say, *Amen*.

CHAPTER 3

Bible Stories

Your word is a lamp to my feet and a light to my path.

Psalm 119:105

Once when I forgot to bring a chapter book for Peter, then six, to read in church (which was in those days essential to his being willing to sit through a service), I grabbed a children's Bible off the shelf in my office. There he sat in the front pew, quietly and fully absorbed in his reading. He began with Creation and read straight through to Samson and Delilah, at which point he turned to me and whispered fiercely, "Mom! This book is *full* of people making bad choices!" This is perhaps the single best reason to read the Bible with your children: from the very beginning God has used deeply flawed, wildly inappropriate, very human people in order to accomplish God's work. If that isn't good news for all of us, I don't know what is. This is still how God works, in and through us.

Let me note, however, that the Bible is in no way a rule-book for life. Yes, I said that, and I will say it again: the Bible is in no way a rulebook for life. The Bible is complicated, contradictory, violent, and misogynistic. It's also beautiful, poetic, wise, and inspiring. Reading the Bible will make you gnash your teeth and pull your hair. Sometimes you will slam it down or even want to throw it across the room. Sometimes it will make you weep with joy, thrum with resonance, sigh with longing. Reading the Bible is challenging. Reading the Bible with children is even more challenging. You are up to this challenge.

If the Bible is not a rulebook for life, then what is it? The Bible is not even a single book at all. Think of it as a library: a collection of more than sixty books written in many different genres, in three different languages on three different continents by many different people over the span of hundreds of years. Long before any of it was written down, before there was even an alphabet, the oldest of these stories were told under a canopy of stars around campfires in the desert. Much later, stories of the life of Jesus were told in house churches during the meal, but first they must have been told around the family table: "Did you hear? Do you remember?" If stories tell us who we are, Bible stories tell us whose we are. It is the story of God seeking and finding God's people, and of God's people seeking and finding God.

Reading the Bible

How do we read the Bible? I suggest we read it carefully and deliberately, thoughtfully, curiously. Author and Episcopalian

Madeleine L'Engle once wrote, "I take the Bible too seriously to take it all literally."[1] That's a very Anglican approach, in fact. For centuries we have understood that the interpretation of scripture is something in which everyone participates: clergy and laypeople, scholars and the rest of us—kids and adults. We use reason, experience, and tradition to help us understand what God might be saying to us today through these ancient texts.[2] Some of it isn't at all relevant. Much of the Bible tells us more about human nature than it does about God. If you grew up with an authoritative view of the Bible or a literal understanding of it, you might want to read *Permission Granted: Take the Bible into Your Own Hands* by biblical scholar Jennifer Grace Bird. She has a "litmus test" that she uses whenever she engages scripture: "If a biblical passage or theological doctrine endorses freedom, liberation, love, the fullness of life for all people, or a mature and responsible faith, then it is 'of God.'"[3] That's the lens she reads scripture through, she's careful to point out. Each of us has our own. Bird reminds us, "The Bible is not God. The Bible was intended to point us toward God."[4]

At about the same age Peter discovered just how complex the Bible is, my book-loving boy was encouraged to learn to ride a bike. After crashing in the driveway he told me firmly, "I prefer safety over fun." In reading, however, he threw caution to the wind. He devoured fantasies, myths, and legends, and was for a long time far more interested in Greek and Roman gods than "your God, Mom, no offense." I wasn't worried, although I confess I was occasionally embarrassed in public settings, as when he casually said just this at dinner one night with a chaplain from Cambridge University.

I thought he might be drawn to the drama and action of the Hebrew Scriptures. As it turned out, it was the very idea of God working in and through us that grew in Peter, and what he found most compelling were the stories of Jesus, God-with-us.

Children's Bibles

We read from various children's bibles at home. There are bibles for children, and then there are storybook bibles that are retellings of some of the Bible. You'll likely want both. I am very picky. Look for beautiful illustrations and remember that Jesus was a Middle Eastern man who was not blue-eyed and blond-haired. Desmond Tutu's *Children of God Storybook Bible* is great for kids in preschool through first grade. For elementary-aged kids I particularly love *The Bible For Children* retold by Murray Watts, and *Shine On: A Story Bible* with questions and activities for young readers. The one I grabbed off my shelf was *The Children's Illustrated Bible* by Selina Hastings, which is chock-full of historical and archeological facts, photographs and maps. A brand-new book that should be on your child's bookshelf or bedside table is *Miracle Man: The Story of Jesus* by the gifted illustrator John Hendrix.

There are also children's bibles to avoid or throw out. Be very careful: some will editorialize in significant ways. Throughout the chapters of *The Children's Adventure Bible,* a complete translation in the New International Version, you'll find colorful boxes decorated with a friendly-looking parrot asking "Did You Know?" which give opinions disguised as facts. In the Book of Revelation, for example (a book of apocalyptic literature which by the way nearly didn't make it into the canon of Holy Scripture at all), these boxes offer subjective and dangerous theological views like, "When it is time to judge the world, Jesus will come back as a warrior with all the armies of heaven,"[5] and, "People who do not believe in Jesus will be in the lake of fire" to be "punished there forever."[6] Know what it means in *The Jesus Storybook Bible*, when Sally Lloyd-Jones writes, "Every story whispers His name."[7] She is saying Jesus is being intentionally read into the Hebrew Scriptures as their fulfillment. Even when we use the phrase "Old Testament," we are implying that the New Testament has completed and surpassed it. This is a valid Christian viewpoint, but it is not the only one. Nothing about the way we interact with scripture should be incidental or accidental.

Wondering Together

Using the method set forth in *Godly Play*, a wonderful Montessori-based program of Christian formation,[8] Peter and I wondered about what we read. We asked, "What part of the story do you like best? What part of the story do you think is the most important? Which part of this story is also about you?" Wondering leads to reflection in ways that often surprise and enrich us, deepening and strengthening our connection to God. Elizabeth Caldwell's new and helpful book for parents is in fact called *I Wonder: Engaging a Child's Curiosity About the Bible*. Wondering is such a natural way into these foundational stories of our faith. They have been sparking our imaginations and stirring our spirits for thousands of years.

We wondered at a picnic about how five thousand people might be fed and during a storm about the calm Jesus brought. Jesus taught and sometimes the people listening just didn't get it—is there anything more relatable to a school-aged child than that? His friends, the disciples, were sometimes great and sometimes disappointing, silly in some situations and at other times brave. Jesus calls God "Father" and the word in Hebrew is more like "Daddy." What does that tell us about how close they were? Then there are the stories Jesus tells, parables—puzzles really: gifts that must be carefully unwrapped to discover their meanings. Each time we read them we may find new meanings. We wondered most about the kingdom of God Jesus describes, already present and not-yet-here: Where do we find it? How do we help it come about?

Responding to the Scriptures

Reading the stories and wondering aloud about them is just a starting point. Kids will want to respond in other ways, too. Peter at three was playing in the bath one night with a toy boat and a blue plastic whale when I heard him intone loudly, "Go to Ninevah!" after hearing the story of Jonah in Sunday school. Acting out the stories is a perennial favorite. The first play I ever directed and starred in was the Nativity in our living room: I was Mary, my brother was Joseph, and my baby doll swaddled in a pale blue flannel receiving blanket was Jesus. We had just come home from the pageant at church. You might start keeping a box of costumes and props. Scarves can be turned into almost anything. Hollywood movies of Bible stories are for the most part disappointing (although *Godspell* and *Jesus Christ Superstar* are in a league of their own) but this should not discourage older kids from making their own videos or podcasts.

How else can you invite your kids to respond to scripture? Open-ended creative responses may be the most worthwhile in stirring spirituality, but sometimes it can be hard to get started if this is a new practice in your family. Make some suggestions at first: a burning bush out of chenille sticks and tissue paper, the tablets Moses carried down from Mount Sinai out of clay, a tambourine like the one Miriam danced with at the parting of the Red Sea from a pie tin.

There is a *Godly Play* tradition of making bookmarks that are illustrative of the stories read to place inside the Bible: my collection includes a rainbow for the story of Noah and a shepherd's crook for the parable of the Good Shepherd. Tell the Genesis stories in the garden and plant there. Kinetic sand works too, if you can't be outdoors. Another *Godly Play* method to bring home is using a "desert box" of sand to tell many of the stories from the Hebrew Scriptures. My friend Emily Given has a terrific book, *Building Faith Brick by Brick* that will give your child "blueprints" for responding to the Bible with LEGO blocks. Build a model of the city of Jerusalem using cardboard boxes. I collect ideas like this on a Pinterest board.

Get some calligraphy pens for kids age eight and older; let them choose a favorite line from the story to copy out and illustrate. Look at illuminated manuscripts at a museum or online (the lavishly decorated ninth-century *Book of Kells* which contains all four Gospels in Latin can be viewed entirely on the website of Trinity College Dublin).[9] You could also watch the gorgeously animated but not religious film, *The Secret of Kells*. To make your own illuminated letters you will need gel pens and metallic Sharpies. Provide creamy heavy-weight paper, textured water color paper, high-quality paints, and colored artists' pencils. Whatever medium or method interests your child is worth trying. The Bible should be as alive in our children's imaginations as fairy tales and *Star Wars*.

Some people write in books and others are scandalized by the thought of it. By the time I was in high school my first bible, presented to me in third grade Sunday school, was full of tiny pictures I'd made as well as margin notes and favorite passages underlined in brightly colored Flair felt-tip pens. Dried flowers and prayers written on index cards were tucked between the pages. Ask grandparents and godparents to show your kids their bibles, their favorite psalms or parables, and notice the variety and the similarities. Now there are bibles made just for journaling and books to tell you how and which pens to use! You could encourage your kids to do the same, or give them a journal for writing down their questions and thoughts, drawings and doodles. This, too, is sacred.

Bible Translations

Now that Peter is older we read different translations of the same passage, comparing the King James Version to the New Revised Standard Version to the Common English Bible to

The Message. The New Revised Standard Version is what we hear most often read on Sundays in Episcopal churches. The Common English Bible is a new translation and very accessible for all ages—if you do not have a Bible at home I recommend getting this one. *The Message* is a lively paraphrase and well worth reading alongside other translations.

Once in a while, reading aloud something from the magnificent King James Version of 1611 is absolutely worth the effort. It was the third authorized translation of the Bible into English, and the work of forty-seven Anglican scholars over eleven years. On Christmas Eve in 1968, half a billion people listened to the creation story in the King James Version read by the three astronauts then orbiting the moon on Apollo 8. Transcendence, indeed. All these and many other translations are available online at biblegateway.com.

Dig Deeper

Learn something about the context of the passage: Who was this story told to, and why? What was happening in this time and place? It is always okay to say to your child, "I don't know what this means. I don't understand this either." A good study Bible will come in handy for this. *The New Oxford Annotated Bible* and *The HarperCollins Study Bible* are both excellent. There is also a student edition of the Common English Bible with notes written by biblical scholars who also have been youth ministers. I particularly appreciate that the editor, Elizabeth Corrie, makes a point of saying, "This Bible is an invitation, and we hope you accept it. . . . Young people are not just leaders for the future but prophets for the present, with unique insights and perspectives that adults need to hear."[10] Amen to *that*. Teens will also appreciate http://schmoop.com, a website not specifically for Bible commentary but with lively and thoughtful notes on books of the Bible written by doctoral students. For understanding the overarching themes in the Bible as well as exploring individual books of the Bible, take a look at the excellent short animated videos available through *The Bible Project*, a nonprofit committed to understanding the Bible in its historical context and communicating its wisdom for the modern world."[11]

When we read the Bible, we like to use the prompt that Emily Scott, our pastor at St. Lydia's Dinner Church[12] poses after scripture is read: "Share a word or a phrase or an image that struck you in the text." Each time a passage is read we are likely to respond to that prompt differently. We also make connections to or contrasts with our own lives and experiences. At St. Lydia's we stick to telling stories, as they give us more than opinions. In this way we learn about each other and ourselves as we learn about God.

Reading Mark's Gospel

The Gospel of Mark makes a great read-aloud for anyone old enough for *Harry Potter*. Middle school and high school kids will appreciate reading Mark alongside the contemporary graphic novel reimagining of this gospel, *Marked* by Steve Ross.

The earliest and shortest of the gospels, Mark was likely written about thirty to forty years after the crucifixion and resurrection, probably around the time just after the Jewish revolt in Jerusalem and the destruction of the Temple in 70 CE. Written in Greek for a largely Gentile audience, Mark also contains phrases in Jesus's native Aramaic. We can easily imagine the text being performed as some scholars think it was. The narrative of Mark is exciting, fast-paced and verb-driven; in it Jesus is a man of action. He casts out demons, heals the sick, gives sight to the blind, feeds the hungry, challenges the powerful, walks on water, raises the dead. For all the miracles, this gospel is also rich with details of everyday life and ordinary people, even Jesus is made startlingly real: we see him at various times cranky, tired, fierce, tender, practical, unpredictable. At one point in his ministry, the gospel tell us, his family "went out to restrain him, for people were saying, 'He has gone out of his mind.'"[13] This doesn't go over well.

Mark's Jesus is both rebel and mystic, upending convention, and defying nature. Over and over again in Mark, Jesus offers glimpses of the kingdom of God, the ways in which God's justice, mercy, and truth are breaking into the world. The dramatic arc of the story relies on the mystery of who Jesus is and what he came to do as well as on the failure of his disciples to recognize and understand this, which is in part why it remains so fresh and relevant to us today. We are right there with them. This is not a biography or a history in any modern sense of the word—none of the gospels are—but to me it is the most compelling and urgent of them.

Most striking is how Mark's gospel ends, at least in its original form. Early in the morning after the Sabbath ended, the women went to the tomb to prepare Jesus's body for burial, worried about who might help them roll away the stone that sealed it shut. When they arrived, the stone had already been rolled away and inside the tomb was a young man who told them that Jesus had been raised from the dead and that they would see him in Galilee. The narrative ends abruptly with these words: "So they went out and fled from the tomb, for terror and amazement had seized them; and they said nothing to anyone, for they were afraid."[14] It's so clearly not what these women who loved Jesus expected. Resurrection was not part of their plan. My own Christian identity does not hinge on a bodily resurrection, but each time I read this I catch my breath, I feel their shock. What's left in this ending is not understanding, but hope, and in that I am deeply moved and strengthened in my faith.

We have a votive candle Peter decorated with ModPodge and scraps of brightly colored tissue paper. When the candle inside is burning the votive glows like stained glass. For years we lit it whenever we read from the Bible at home. We look for illumination in the Word of God. Sometimes it comes easily, often not. We keep at it. We are People of the Book, and wrestling with these stories is our birthright.

CHAPTER 4

Why Church?

✝

For where two or three are gathered in my name,
I am there among them. Matthew 18:20

The simple answer to the question, "Why go to church?" is that we are not Christians alone. Despite what some well-meaning people will tell you, Christianity is not about a personal relationship with Jesus. Christian life by necessity, almost by definition, is one lived in community. We *need* each other. The first Christians, remember, did not identify themselves as such. They were followers of the Way, trying to live as Jesus did. They gathered in homes, shared a common meal, read scripture, told the stories that Jesus told, took care of each other, shared their resources with those among them who were in need.[1] "The community measured faithfulness by how well its members practiced loving God and neighbor. Not offering hospitality was a much greater failing than not believing Jesus was 'truly God' and 'truly human.'"[2] There was no church yet, no beautiful building with soaring arches and glowing stained glass, or whatever you picture when you hear that word. *The community* was the Church.

Finding a Church Home

To be clear, when we talk about the Church with a capital c, we are always talking about people, not the building. *We* are the Church, the body of Christ, everyone who tries to follow Jesus, full stop. Let's also be clear that since the time of Jesus, there has never been a Golden Age where all Christians everywhere agreed on what to think or believe. We've been fighting amongst ourselves from the beginning. So let's put aside who has it right about God and Jesus. We aren't going to solve that today. I hope you already have a church where you and your family feel at home. (My family has at least four, but we are weird that way.) If you don't, here's what I look for:

Open Doors, Open Hearts, Open Minds

The first act of Jesus's public ministry was to call disciples. Jesus gathered a community, and let all kinds of people in. People who made others feel uncomfortable, people the religious leaders avoided and even rejected. That's why God's table often looks different from ours: everyone's included. I am most comfortable in a church where I see diversity: a mix of ages, races, and socio-economic backgrounds. I am even learning to be comfortable with diversity in beliefs. My own Christian faith skirts the edge much of the time. I struggle with the divinity of Christ, but the human Jesus draws me closer. I go to church and work with many who are less heretical than I. They love me anyway.

Women in Leadership and at the Altar

This is really important to me: I never heard that women could not be leaders in the church, and to be fair, the church I grew up in had the strong example of a highly creative and devout woman, Barbara Mudge. She was my Sunday school teacher and the director of religious education. She was also my elementary school teacher for three consecutive years because she had found another way of ministering. The summer I was fourteen, the Episcopal Church voted to allow the ordination of women, and a few years later, my beloved teacher was the first woman in our county to be ordained an Episcopal priest. Never have I known someone so obviously called to the priesthood as she was. Never has anyone been Jesus to me as much as she was. Her ordination was so joyful, and it was for me a righting of an ancient wrong, since "There is no longer Jew or Greek, there is no longer slave or free, there is no longer male and female; for all of you are one in Christ Jesus."[3]

Women were clearly leaders in the early church, given a level of authority that was in stark contrast to what most women experienced in first century Israel and Rome. Jesus welcomed women as equals, and yet, for every woman mentioned in the New Testament, how many were edited out by disapproving scribes? I am certain the reason the disciples didn't believe at first in Jesus's resurrection was that Mary Magdalene witnessed it first. We haven't ended misogyny in the church, but we have had forty years of prophetic leadership by ordained women in our tradition, and for that I am deeply grateful.

Church That Extends beyond the Walls

I have been quoting this line for a long time, but I can't for the life of me find where it comes from: "Church isn't just Sundays, it's seven days a week. We bring the church with us." There are lots of great things that happen in church on Sundays—worship, education, fellowship, service. We can't leave it there, though. We must go into the world—or at least into our own neighborhoods and cities. The church is not a club. As William Temple (1881–1944) famously said, "The church is the only institution that exists for the benefit of those who are not its members." Some churches call this outreach, being of service to those we can reach out to, near and far. We don't *go* to church, we *are* the Church.

A Liturgical Church

Belonging to a liturgical church is my strong personal bias, and there are many other inclusive, nourishing faith communities outside this tradition. Catholics, Episcopalians, and Lutherans all participate in liturgy, "the work of the people," a pattern of public worship with ancient origins that includes singing, praying, reading and responding to scripture, and Holy Eucharist, sometimes called Holy Communion. The rhythm of the service is largely the same from week to week and from place to place within the cycle of the church year. The style of worship may be traditional or contemporary, the services may be short or long, but in the liturgy we find beauty, mystery, and the presence of God.

Children Everywhere . . .

Children should be seen and heard, full participants in the life of the church. Steam shoots out of my ears whenever I am told "children are the future of the Church." Children are the Church right now, and without them we are incomplete.

Worshiping with Children

Once you have found a church, please go. Don't feel guilty about not going every week; almost no one does that anymore. Go when you can, schedule around it. Consistency will help. You'll be tempted to sit in the back, especially if you think your kids might be disruptive. Ignore that impulse and sit up front, where they can see. There's a lot of dramatic action in liturgical churches and your children will be drawn to it. Don't be afraid to whisper in their ears, narrating the action as it happens. Good liturgy is a feast for the senses. Point to the songs in the hymnal, help readers follow along in the bulletin. People may from time to time give you dirty looks. Smile at them and report it to the clergy—it's their problem, not yours, I promise you. Children belong in church. Aside from having parents who are active in and talk about their faith, the biggest indicator of children who grow into an adult faith is participation in worship.[4]

Life in the Pew

Your children will sometimes make noise, wiggle, and drop hymnals with a loud thud. That's okay. They're children. Give them paper and crayons. Pew art is not a distraction, Gretchen Pritchard notes, "It helps children to listen."[5] We also need to give them a visual vocabulary. These images of God from the conversations you have at home, read about in the Bible, and encounter in nature and in life will help them get beyond hearts and crosses: "Whatever we help them to *see* and to *draw*, we are also helping them to think about and understand, to remember, recognize, and work with: we are providing them with tools for theological thought, for devotion, prayer and ultimately, moral choice and personal growth."[6]

You could pack a "quiet bag" with special items just for Sundays: board books with a spiritual theme or a children's Bible, quiet age-appropriate toys or activities such as a soft stuffed lamb or a flat Jesus (inspired by *Flat Stanley*), a small container of play dough or modeling beeswax, or a finger labyrinth.[7]

Leadership Roles

If you volunteer to usher or greet people as they arrive, your children can help you do that. Perhaps they are old enough to be acolytes who assist the clergy in worship, carrying the cross or the torches or helping to set the altar. Maybe there is a children's choir—truly, this is what has kept Peter active and mostly happy in church all these years. He has also long loved serving as a lector (reading the lesson) or intercessor (reading the prayers) and at thirteen just preached his first sermon. (He was shocked by the invitation from our dinner church, St. Lydia's. "Don't blame me if I cause the Apocalypse," he told us—but he said yes.)

Sacraments

Liturgical churches are also sacramental churches. The Book of Common Prayer defines a sacrament as "an outward and visible sign of an inward and spiritual grace."[8] In the Episcopal Church we have two great sacraments given to us by Jesus: baptism and communion.

Holy Baptism

Baptism is "full initiation by water and the Holy Spirit into Christ's Body the Church."[9] Jesus was baptized at the beginning of his ministry by his cousin John in the Jordan River, and as he came out of the water, the people who were there that day saw a dove come down from heaven, and heard the voice of God say, "This is my Son, the Beloved, with whom I am well pleased."[10] This is what God says to each of us on our baptismal day: "You are my beloved child, and I am so happy with you." This is the story to whisper in your child's ear over and over. This is how we begin our Christian life.

We baptize people at every age and stage of life. We baptize infants and children too young to make these promises for themselves not because they need "fire insurance,"[11] but because we understand that they already belong to God and that we, their parents and godparents, are responsible for seeing that they are "brought up in the Christian faith and life."[12] We promise to turn away from evil, to turn toward

Jesus, and everyone present renews their own commitment to do just that. Private baptisms, once the norm, are now rare. The entire congregation promises to do all in their power "to uphold these persons in their life in Christ" and joins in the extraordinary promises we make next. We are not Christians alone.

The Baptismal Covenant begins with the Apostles' Creed, what my friend Helen Barron calls an "imaginative rendition of truths too huge to compress into succinct words." She suggests reading it as "a love song we sing back to 'God the Father, God the Son and God the Holy Spirit.'"[13] The second half of the Baptismal Covenant is a set of five promises, always made "with God's help." The first promise has to do with coming to church, so there's *that*: "Will you continue in the apostles' teaching and fellowship, in the breaking of bread and in the prayers?" The next two are also familiar and fair: "Will you persevere in resisting evil and whenever you fall into sin, repent and return to the Lord?" (I especially appreciate "whenever" here; yes, we fall short and miss the mark all the time. Then we turn around and try again.) "Will you proclaim by word and example the good news of God in Christ?" Gospel means "good news," and another favorite quote of mine attributed to St. Francis of Assisi works well here: "Preach the Gospel at all times, and if necessary use words." What we do is so much more important than what we say. The last two promises are so audacious in their scope that it takes my breath away each time I hear them: "Will you seek and serve Christ in all persons, loving your neighbor as yourself?" and "Will you strive for justice and peace among all people and respect the dignity of every human being?" What a challenge! What an opportunity! Thank God we have the rest of our lives to work on these. This is what it means to follow Jesus.

The symbols of baptism are powerful and rich with meaning. Water is the source of life and necessary for life. All the water that ever will be already exists: the water that rocked the ark, the water that parted before Moses, the water that flowed from Jesus's side is the very same water that we use for bathing, laundry, washing up the dishes, filling the kiddy pool, and watering the basil on the window sill. The water that puts out the campfire and the house fire, the water that drips from my Brooklyn tap and floods low-lying land, the water from the well in Kenya and the mud puddle in Cambodia and the water in the font at your child's baptism is the water that has been here since the beginning of time. All water is holy water.

After the water comes oil that water cannot dissolve. The priest makes a cross of oil on the forehead of the newly baptized. Oil was used to anoint prophets and priests in the Hebrew Scriptures (Old Testament); "Christ" means, "anointed one." Oil was used in healing and we still use it to anoint the sick and the dying. This oil, called chrism, marks us as "Christ's own forever." It is a bond, sealing a promise.

The last symbol of baptism is light. The paschal candle reminds us of the resurrection, of the light that cannot be extinguished even by death. Jesus is the light of the world and through baptism we are Christ's light in the world. The light that shines in us, which we see so clearly in our children and in acts of love, kindness, and generosity every day is the light that allows us to see God in others, and allows others to see God in us. Let your light so shine. . . .

Holy Eucharist

The Eucharist is what we do when we gather on Sundays in most liturgical churches around the world. The service[14] has two parts, the Liturgy of the Word and the Liturgy of the Table. In the first part, we praise God and pray to God. We hear the Word of God read in lessons from the Bible, usually one from the Hebrew Scriptures, then a psalm, followed by a reading from the letters or "epistles" in the New Testament (or in the Easter season from the Acts of the Apostles), and always a reading from one of the four gospels. The preacher responds to the readings in a sermon. We affirm our faith by saying together one of the creeds, and prayer is offered on behalf of all who are gathered, for the Church, the nation, the world, the local community, those in need, and those who have died.

Often we make a confession of sin together, asking God's forgiveness for "what we have done and left undone," for not loving God "with our whole heart" and not loving "our neighbors as ourselves." We do this to remind ourselves that while we may never fully succeed at this, we keep trying. We are forgiven. Then the Peace of God is offered to all. We shake hands with or even embrace those around us, making peace with each other before the Liturgy of the Table begins. At God's table we are all equals, sharing in God's grace.

The second half of the service begins with the offertory. Money collected from the congregation is brought forward along with the bread and the wine and sometimes other gifts as well, such as canned and boxed food that will be given to a local pantry. The word "eucharist" means thanksgiving. We give thanks to God for the gifts of God, returning to

God a part of what we have been given. We give thanks for God's acts in human history, and for Jesus, who reconciles us to God.

Next we reenact the last supper Jesus shared with the disciples. We hear the words Jesus spoke to them: "Do this in remembrance of me." The priest then calls on the power of the Holy Spirit to make the bread and wine holy and make us holy, too. Just before we share the broken bread and common cup, we say together the Lord's Prayer. This is when we come close to God's kingdom "on earth as it is in heaven;" this is the feast where all who are hungry share in the meal. We use the words "Christ's body and blood," which seem strange and primitive. What we mean, I think, is that this is an act at once deeply intimate and universal, physical and mystical. Once, I stood with a six-year-old a few feet away from the priest as he broke the large, round "host." Jack, who had been baptized earlier in the service, was new to our church. "Is that the bread everyone eats?" he asked me. "Does it taste good?" Not wanting to lie, I whispered back, "It's not so tasty, but it's very special. That bread is Jesus for us, and when we eat it, we have Jesus inside us." Jack gave a nod and whispered back with urgency, "I *want* that bread."

Communion and community have the same root. It is worth noting that a priest does not celebrate the Eucharist if they are alone. It is a communal act. In the bread and wine "we are united with God and with one another" and from this we are sent out into the world "to do the work God has given us to do." We now have been given the "strength and courage" we need to do it. As some church bulletins note, "The worship is over. The service begins."

A word about children receiving communion: YES. What happens in communion is a mystery to all of us regardless of age or maturity. Gretchen Pritchard says, "We don't really know why a kiss on the cheek feels like love. All the more, we do not know why bread and wine feel like Christ. . . . Children who have been fed at the Lord's table since earliest infancy are like children who have had plenty of hugs and kisses—they need hardly to be taught about God's love in bread and wine because they already know all about it; they feel it in their bones."[15] This is a practice of the early church to which we have returned.

Confirmation

The carrot of communion was for ages why young people in Episcopal churches got confirmed; that is, they made for themselves the promises their parents and godparents made on their behalf in baptism, became full members of the church, and were then admitted to receive communion. However, since the adoption of the latest revision to the Book of Common Prayer in 1979 (and reverting back to those early Church practices), we acknowledge that baptism is full membership (and initiation) into Christ's Church.

Although confirmation is no longer a rite of entrance to communion or membership, we still confirm youth in the Episcopal Church, and it is still a public affirmation of faith following a period of study and reflection. The bishop lays hands on those being confirmed with a prayer invoking the power of the Holy Spirit to strengthen and sustain them for service. That's what Episcopal means, by the way: the *episco-*

pacy refers to our bishops, who are linked through history by the laying-on-of-hands to the first apostles.

Confirmation is not required, and it must be something one chooses freely. I remind parents and youth that we call this a journey of faith, and confirmation is a milestone on this journey, not an endpoint. It can be a great opportunity for teens to decide what new role or responsibility they will take on in church or in the community as a way of living out the Baptismal Covenant. I tell every young person I help guide through this process that in order to be confirmed, they do not need to have the right answers; in fact, I expect them to have more questions at the end of the confirmation process than they had at the start. In the Rite of Confirmation, what they are promising is that this story, our Christian story, is the one they will keep wrestling with for the rest of their lives. As Rilke wrote to the young poet, I hope we "try to love the questions themselves" so we can "live [our] way into the answer."[16]

The Episcopal Church

This is the denomination that formed me. We are part of the worldwide Anglican Communion, which has more than 80 million members in 165 countries.[17] We trace our history to the very beginning of the Christian church in 33 CE. The Church of England was founded in 597 as an outpost of the Roman Catholic Church and broke with it in 1534 for a variety of reasons. (You may have heard that it was because the Pope wouldn't give Henry VIII a divorce, but trust me, it's a bit more complicated than that.) We are the middle road—the *via media*—between Roman Catholicism and Protestantism. During the American Revolution, we separated from the Church of England and became The Episcopal Church.

We are governed by a combination of bishops, priests, deacons, and laypeople elected by local church members. All churches that have ties to the Anglican Communion have a Book of Common Prayer that guides our worship and teachings. We believe God is still speaking to us, and we discern what God is saying to us using scripture, reason, and tradition.

Putting Faith into Action

We are a mildly activist family, and I have the church to thank for that. I cannot separate my political beliefs from my religious beliefs. For me, it is all of a piece. The first time I left Peter overnight was to participate in an interfaith prayer service at the National Cathedral in Washington, D.C. on the eve of the 2004 presidential election at the invitation of Marian Wright Edelman of The Children's Defense Fund. I told her, "Mrs. Edelman, if I am not able to be there, it's because I am the only parent of a twenty-month-old." She put her hand firmly on my shoulder and said, "My dear, that's precisely why you *will be* there." She was right.

When I was growing up, the Episcopal Church in our Diocese of Los Angeles boycotted Nestlé because, my mother explained, they were marketing baby formula in third world countries and as a result, babies were dying. Hearing that, and not making or eating chocolate chip cookies for a time had a significant impact on me as a child. The boycott of green grapes in support of California's migrant farm workers also had an impact on my school lunch box. Our church, St. Mary's, in Laguna Beach, California, turned its rectory over to a family of Vietnamese refugees.

Until I was in my late teens, I certainly thought every church had gay and lesbian families. Peter was five when the California Supreme Court struck down the ban on same-sex marriage. The church where I worked celebrated the momentous occasion with a champagne toast and wedding cake, and I brought Peter over from the children's center next door to join in the festivities. "Now Jann and Kathy can get married!" I told him excitedly, referring to our dear friends. "What do you mean?" Peter asked, aghast. "Jann and Kathy *couldn't* get married before?" It simply had never occurred to him.

Peter has carried signs at anti-war rallies and was once among the youngest participants at the United Nations official observance of the International Day of Peace. He has marched with friends in support of the Black Lives Matter movement. He's heard Bryan Stevenson, author of *Just Mercy,* speak about the school-to-prison pipeline and watched Anna Deveare Smith transform herself into a dozen different people, each offering a challenging perspective on race in America. All of these are opportunities that have come through our lives in the church. Everything that's worth talking about with our kids is worth talking about in the context of our faith.

What I love most about being an Episcopalian is summed up in the prayer for the newly baptized. We ask God to give them "an inquiring and discerning heart, the courage to will and to persevere, a spirit to know and love you, and the gift of joy and wonder in all your works."[18] With that, and with God, *anything* is possible.

CHAPTER 5

Seasons and Celebrations

For everything there is a season. . . . Ecclesiastes 3:1

N ew Year's Day is on January 1. In New York City the
school year begins in September, around the same time
our Jewish friends celebrate Rosh Hashanah, the Jewish New
Year. Chinese New Year is in February. Our upstairs neighbors observe the Persian New Year as spring begins. I relish
all these opportunities for fresh starts and take advantage of
them as often as possible.

The Church's new year comes late in the secular calendar. Christians mark time in a different way. Following the
liturgical cycle of seasons and holy days can create a faith-
filled home and set a rhythm and a pattern that helps us

make meaning in our lives through the stories and traditions handed down from generation to generation.

Advent

The Christian liturgical calendar begins in late fall with the first Sunday of **Advent**, which means "coming." In the secular world this period of preparing for the birth of Christ has been swept up into "the holiday season," that frantic period of time from just after Halloween (if we're lucky) until Christmas Eve. In the church, however, we are serious about getting ready over a four-week period. The color of Advent is blue (for Mary, the mother of Jesus) or purple (for the newborn king). The evergreen wreaths we make at church are horizontal, to place on a table with four candles set into them, one to be lighted each week. No carols are sung; the mood is quiet, simple, more focused. We are waiting for Jesus, and this is holy time. This slower, more deliberate approach to the season may be worth bringing home. What can you simplify? Where can you be more intentional, less rushed?

Christmas and Epiphany

Christmas Eve is when churches are at their very best. The colors on the altar and vestments worn by the clergy are white for joy and gold for celebration. Go, see the baby lying in a manger (if there isn't a pageant, there surely will be a crèche), sing the angels' song of peace, and expect that your children will want to tell the story over and over again when you get home. You may have a beautiful crèche or nativity set that you will not want your kids to play with, so—if you can—get another that's sturdy or unbreakable. It's worth it. The story of Christmas is one with great power over our hearts and imaginations, and it's natural that we want to get our hands on it.

Perhaps keeping Advent at home is not helpful to you. It is not currently helpful in our house. As someone who works full time in the church, December is an incredibly busy month for me, so reality dictates that the tree goes up when there's time—and some years that's Thanksgiving weekend. However, we take full advantage of knowing that there are twelve days of Christmas and the first day is Christmas Day. That's right—just when everyone else thinks Christmas is over, my family is just beginning to celebrate. Our holiday party is the Saturday after Christmas, and sometimes the cookie baking waits until then, too.

Save one gift for each person to open on January 6, the **Feast of the Epiphany**, when we remember the visit of the Magi to the child Jesus. This part of the story is one that bears closer attention. Though in most Christmas pageants, three kings arrive just after the shepherds bearing gifts for the baby, that's not what the Bible actually says. Read the story in Matthew's gospel (1:18–2:7) and wonder: What's up with those gifts of gold, frankincense, and myrrh? Collect some gently used baby clothes, new diapers, and formula to take to a women's shelter; babysit for a friend, offering a much-needed break to the parent and some insight into what it means that God came to us not just in human form, but as a baby, born helpless and dependent as all babies are, to a poor family in a troubled place.

Winter Saints

Let me say a word about the saints. The Book of Common Prayer calls saints "the lights of the world in every generation"—people whose lives and deeds have shone brightly and helped others more closely follow Jesus. There are saints who lived long ago and there are saints living and working in the world today, saints who are known by the church and saints who are known only to God. We say that we are part of the Communion of Saints, the company of all faithful people, connected through our baptism to those Christians who have died, those who are alive now, and those yet to be born. The word "saint" means holy. In the Episcopal Church we have a Calendar of Saints, holy men and women we remember in prayer and with readings from scripture on their feast day. The saints tend to be quite colorful, and being perfect is in no way a requirement.

The Feast of St. Nicholas

Nicholas of Myra was born in what is now western Turkey in the latter part of the second century. His feast day is in early Advent, December 6. The most famous story told about Nicholas is one that may have inspired the story of Santa Claus. There was a poor family with three daughters. In those days young women could not be married unless they had dowries, sums of money that were to be given to their husbands. On each of three nights, a sack of gold was tossed into their home through an open window, landing in their shoes—or in their stockings hanging by the fire to dry. These gifts, given in secret, saved the young women from being sold into slavery. If you place an orange or a clementine in the toe of your child's Christmas stocking, this is the reason: it represents Nicholas's gift of gold.

Stories are also told of Nicholas protecting children and sailors, feeding the hungry in Myra during two years of famine, and going before the Emperor Constantine to ask for lower taxes for his people. He also attended the Council of Nicea, the first great meeting of bishops from all over the Christian world in 325, from which we get the Nicene Creed that we say together in church on Sundays.

Nicholas is remembered especially in Europe, Greece, and Russia. On the evening of December 5, children leave hay and carrots in their shoes for St. Nicholas's horse and wake to find that they've been exchanged for small toys or chocolates. People all over the world honor St. Nicholas during Advent and Christmas by being generous to those in need, and by giving gifts in secret.

How might your family continue the tradition of gift giving in secret? Our church in California has an "angel tree" hung with tags filled out by children and teens in the foster care system with what they most want for Christmas. The year Peter was three and a half, we choose the tag of a boy the same age who wanted the very same gift as Peter: Thomas the Tank Engine. Then we went shopping. Peter asked, "Doesn't Santa come to every house?" I answered, "No, we have to help." Peter asked with great excitement, "You mean *we* get to be Santa for Julio?"

You can have an Angel Tree at home, too. A lovely picture book with ideas for giving to others in this season is LuAnn Schnable Kaldor's *The Angels On My Tree.* You could start a

53

collection of angel ornaments and put one on the tree each time your family participates in an act of kindness to others, or you could make angel ornaments and start a collection that way. There are several simple patterns on my Pinterest board, which are linked on my blog, wendyclairebarrie.com.

Martin Luther King, Jr.

The church for centuries has observed the feasts of saints on the day of their death, but in this case, please celebrate the ministry of the Reverend Dr. Martin Luther King, Jr. when our nation does, on the Monday closest to January 15, his birthday. What your kids learn about him in school isn't enough: his Christian faith and his calling compelled Dr. King to make civil rights his life's work.

The lesson from the Hebrew Scriptures appointed for his feast day is taken from the story of Joseph with the coat of many colors, whose brothers were jealous of him and decided to get rid of him. Eventually, they sold him into slavery, but Joseph became a powerful leader in Egypt. Pharaoh, Egypt's king, believed Joseph's dreams and because of that, Joseph was able to save the Egyptians and even his own brothers from a terrible famine. It is taken from Genesis 37:17–20:

They said to one another, "Here comes this dreamer. Come now, let us kill him and throw him into one of the pits; then we shall say that a wild animal has devoured him, and we shall see what will become of his dreams."

Read or listen to the "I Have a Dream" speech, beginning at the line, "I have a dream that one day this nation will rise up and live out the true meaning of its creed: 'we hold these truths to be self-evident, that all men are created equal."'[1] Continue to the end of the speech. Talk as a family about Dr. King's dream, and how it has continued after his death.

Many people across the country take this day as a day of service. How can your family participate in making his dream come true? This is one of my favorite quotes of Dr. King: "Life's most persistent and urgent question is, 'What are you doing for others?'"

Families with young children could try beginning this conversation with a brown egg and a white egg. Crack the eggs into the bowl one at a time. No matter what we look like on the outside, inside we are the same. Dr. King's most famous speech is about his dream that everyone will one day live the way God wants us to live, treating each other fairly and with love, no matter the color of our skin or how different we might be. Read this quote: "I have a dream that my four little children will one day live in a nation where they will not be judged by the color of their skin but by the content of their character." What we have inside us is the most important part of us. Talk together about what we dream of doing to make the world a better (peaceful, fairer) place. Read the excellent picture book *God's Dream* by Desmond Tutu.

Valentine's Day

There is no historical basis for a saint called Valentine and the story we have about him is rather gruesome, but that shouldn't keep you from making February 14 all about love. Include strangers: fill up snack-sized Ziploc bags with chocolate hearts or kisses and hide them for others to find. Make valentines from colored construction paper or from paper that you might have recycled which you can brush with red, pink, and purple watercolor. Take extra and signed valentines to the public library and tuck them into books.

Peter was due on February 12. On February 14 I woke up feeling huge and miserable, like this baby was going to stay inside me forever. The weather had been below freezing for several days. I looked out the window of my New York City apartment and discovered that someone had hung a large red tag-board heart decorated with glitter and shiny stickers that caught the light in the branches of every tree on our block. Even though they were not meant for me personally, those valentines made me feel loved. Read *Somebody Loves You, Mr. Hatch* by Eileen Spinelli and dream up acts of kindness for your neighbors. God's love spills over into everything and everyone if we let it.

Lent

Shrove Tuesday

Better known as Mardi Gras or Fat Tuesday, Shrove Tuesday is the day before Lent begins. In the Middle Ages, people used up all the fat in the house—butter, milk, eggs, meat—on the night before Lent began so that they could come closer to God by giving up these foods as they prepared for the great feast of Easter. Pancakes are traditional in England for this, so Episcopalians often have breakfast for dinner, while those celebrating Mardi Gras are likely eating gumbo and Kings' Cake. What kings, you ask? The Magi—the ones who brought gifts to the holy child at Epiphany.

Ash Wednesday

Ash Wednesday is not a day many people take their children to church, since these are the words we hear when we receive the cross of ashes on our foreheads: "Remember that you are dust, and to dust you shall return."[2] The cross of oil given to us in the same place at our baptism is made with the words (in the Episcopal Church), "You are sealed by the Holy Spirit in Baptism and marked as Christ's own forever."[3] We can't hide from our children that being human means that one day we will die, but we can frame it for them in religious terms: "We belong to God and we return to God." It helps me to think of it this way: "From Love we come, and to Love we return."

Lent

Lent, the forty-day season (not including Sundays) in which we prepare for Easter, is a time to come closer to God. The church's color is purple, historically the most expensive dye, because we are waiting for our king. Alternatively, some churches use "Lenten array," rough fabric in a drab color for this penitential season. Many people still mark the season by fasting—giving something up—be it chocolate, Facebook, or video games. When I was growing up, we had meatless Mondays in Lent, but I know a family now who are vegetarian for the full six weeks. My husband has often fasted from judgment in Lent by giving a dollar to everyone who asks, and looking them in the eye as he does so, which is not a common practice in New York City.

We give up something in Lent to make more room for God. You could read the Bible each night before bed, or even one night each week, or choose a book with spiritual resonance for a family read-aloud: *The Lion, the Witch and the Wardrobe* by C.S. Lewis or *A Wrinkle in Time* by Madeleine L'Engle. Try taking on a new prayer practice, such as writing to God. Author Rachel Hackenburg's *Writing to God* comes in two editions, one for adults and one for kids. If that seems like too much, find a box big enough for holding blank index cards. Everyone can write or draw prayers and concerns, hopes and sorrows. Putting them into the box is a way of turning them over to God. Try praying at a particular time of day, like Compline at bedtime.

Another important Lenten practice is giving to others. Jenifer Gamber has a downloadable Lenten calendar on her website http://myfaithmylife.org for "returning God's blessings out into the world" by encouraging families to be mindful of their privileges. One day you might be asked to give twenty-five cents for every bottle of medicine in your house; another day to add a nickel for every time you turn on the water faucet or flush the toilet! The money can go in the collection plate at church, to a local food bank, or to an international relief organization such as UNICEF or Episcopal Relief and Development.

What else can you do? Spend time outdoors. Lent means lengthen—the days are getting longer. Turn off the screens and take walks after dinner. Spend some time each Saturday picking up trash at the park or helping an older neighbor in the yard. Find something that makes sense for your family and try it. It's okay to slip or skip. Try again. God doesn't mind.

Holy Week

All of Lent has been building to this Holy Week, the final week before Easter. The real action is at church, beginning with:

Palm Sunday

We remember how Jesus rode into Jerusalem on the back of a donkey instead of a stallion, speaking of peace instead of leading a great army, and the people waved palms in celebration, as if they were welcoming a king. We wave palms, too. Some of those palms we fold into crosses, and keep in our homes all year until it's time to bring them back to church, where each year they are burned to make the ashes that are used on Ash Wednesday.

Maundy Thursday

On this day, we remember the last supper Jesus shared with his disciples, which may or may not have been a Passover meal. Only John's gospel, however, tells how after dinner, Jesus washed the feet of his disciples, guys who wore sandals on unpaved dirt roads all the time, whose feet must have been filthy. This was a servant's work, and Jesus gave the disciples a new commandment ("mandatum" in Latin): "Love one another as I have loved you."[4] For this reason we churchy people do a strange thing: we wash one another's feet. It's awkward, it's uncomfortable, and I know lots of people who get pedicures first. It's humbling and touching, too. A priest washes the feet of a child who then washes the feet of her mother. A businessman washes the feet of a man who is homeless.

Good Friday

Right. This day is hard for adults, let alone kids, and it's really important to resist skipping over it and going straight to Easter. We do know how the story ends. We call Good Friday "good" because we are an Easter people. Even in the name we give it, we do not look at this day alone for the terrible thing that happened, that Jesus died on the cross. We look all the way to Sunday, when Jesus rose again. Jesus, whom we love, died on a dark day when soldiers shamed him, nearly all his friends left his side, and he wasn't even sure that God was with him. We tell the story of what happened that day because it is vital for our children to hear: Jesus was afraid, he suffered, he died . . . and God turned his fear, his suffering, and his dying into hope, wholeness, and new life.

We tell this story—our Christian story—over and over again because it tells us the truth: not that there is no darkness, but that "light shines in the darkness and the darkness has not overcome it."[5] Remembering that gives us comfort and makes us bold, helps us encourage others and find goodness in the most difficult of days. We are Easter people because we have been to the cross and the grave and we know the promise God makes to us in Jesus: God's power and grace can transform anything; God's love is stronger than the cross, stronger than death itself.

You might bring some sweetness to this bitter day in a traditional way, by baking hot cross buns, a custom that dates to Saxon times. My husband makes this recipe:[6]

HOT CROSS BUNS

Ingredients

1 package active dry yeast
¼ cup warm milk
1 teaspoon sugar

3 cups all purpose flour
¼ cup sugar
½ teaspoon cardamom
½ teaspoon cinnamon
½ teaspoon allspice
¼ teaspoon cloves
¼ teaspoon nutmeg (preferably freshly grated)
1 teaspoon salt

4 tablespoons butter, softened
2 eggs
½ cup warm milk
¾ cup currants
2 teaspoons grated orange zest

1 egg
1 tablespoon milk

1 teaspoon milk
3 to 5 tablespoons powdered sugar
OR, instead of milk and sugar: white chocolate chips

Directions

1. Warm ¼ cup of milk. Stir in 1 teaspoon of sugar and sprinkle in the package of yeast. Let sit 5 to 10 minutes until foamy.

2. In a large bowl, whisk together 3 cups of flour, 1 teaspoon of salt, all the spices and ¼ cup of sugar.

3. Make a well in the flour and add the yeast mixture, 4 tablespoons of melted butter, 2 eggs, and ½ cup warm milk. Mix the ingredients well with a wooden spoon. Mix in the currants and orange zest.

4. Knead until well mixed; knead in additional tablespoons of flour until the dough doesn't stick to your fingers or the bowl.

5. Form the dough into a ball, cover the bowl with plastic wrap and leave at room temperature for 2 hours—the dough should double in size.

6. Press down on the dough to deflate it, then roll into a log and divide into 16 pieces. Form each piece into a bun by rolling between your hands.

7. Place the buns on a baking sheet, at least an inch apart. Cover it all with plastic wrap and let it sit for another 40 minutes, until they've doubled again.

8. Preheat the oven to 400 degrees. Whisk together 1 egg and 1 tablespoon of milk. (Some people use a sharp knife to slash a cross in the top of each bun to guide the icing later, but I prefer the smooth dome.)

9. Brush egg wash on each bun. (Optional but they look a lot better.)

10. Put in the oven on the middle rack and cook for about 12 minutes. Remove from oven, cool a few minutes, then move to a wire rack to cool more.

11. For traditional white frosting, whisk together 1 teaspoon of milk and 3 tablespoons of powdered sugar. Whisk in additional tablespoons of sugar until it's a little thicker

than you think it needs to be. After the buns are *totally* cooled, use an icing bag or a plastic sandwich bag with a corner snipped off to pipe a cross on each bun. You can also use white chocolate instead of white icing. Just melt white chocolate chips in the microwave or over a double boiler, then proceed as above.

Break your fast (yes, that's where the word *breakfast* comes from) with these, and make enough to share with your neighbors or with the overworked staff of your church, who still have these three intense days before they rest.

The Great Vigil on Holy Saturday

The Great Vigil is the holiest night of the year. If you like Midnight Mass on Christmas Eve, you will love the Great Vigil of Easter. TAKE YOUR KIDS. Not preschoolers. I recommend ages eight and up. They can come in their pajamas. The service, elements of which date back to the second century, begins in darkness. A fire is kindled, perhaps outside, perhaps at the back of the church, and from it the paschal candle (a really huge candle) is lit. This candle is such a powerful symbol of the resurrection that it is present for not only every baptism but for every funeral as well, and it will stay lit for every liturgy, every service for all fifty days of Easter. (Yes, fifty! That's how important Easter is to us. It's not just one day, but a season in itself.) The paschal candle is brought into the church with chanting and individual candles are lit from it as the light of Christ spreads throughout the congregation.

By candlelight the stories of God's saving deeds in history are told, always including the Exodus. People are baptized, alleluias are shouted and sung, the lights blaze, bells are rung, the Easter gospel is proclaimed, and everyone is fed with the bread and wine made holy. Talk about a great party!

Easter

Easter Day seems like a quieter affair by contrast—but only by contrast. Wake your children up in the morning with the ages-old acclamation, "Alleluia, Christ is risen!" They will soon learn the response: "The Lord is risen indeed. Alleluia!" Your earliest riser could do this for the family, given a bell to ring through the house. You'll need to get up early to find good seats at church. Churches everywhere go all out with music, flowers, and celebration. This is a quirky story we tell, the resurrection of our Lord. Resurrection means, "to cause to stand up." Easter is an even greater mystery than Christmas. My understanding of the hows and whys is imperfect. What I do believe is that our God is a God of love, grace, and mercy. Wondering how to tie in the egg hunt, the baskets, and the bunny? Don't work too hard at it. Enjoy the festivities, look for signs of new life, be Easter people.

How will you observe Eastertide, the Great Fifty Days? You could raise butterflies, even in an apartment. My most personal experience of resurrection was the year we brought home a caterpillar from the children's museum, when Peter was four. Our tiny friend ate food from a tub they provided, and we painted the inside of a shoebox to look garden-like. A stick wedged at an angle provided a place for the chrysalis to hang, and sure enough, one day our friend began to change. Covered with clear cellophane, the shoebox sat on the baker's rack in our kitchen. For weeks, nothing happened. I was sure we had a dud. I even stopped bringing Peter's attention to it, but I hadn't the heart to throw it out. Then one day we came home to what we thought might be a small earthquake. (We lived in Southern California; it wasn't unlikely.) Peter quickly realized it was just the baker's rack that was shaking. The chrysalis had finally burst and our butterfly was beating its wings against the cellophane! We ran outside and released it. You can well imagine our surprise and joy! It was Easter all over again.

You can order just the caterpillar larvae and food, or spend about $20 and get a reusable 12" pop-up butterfly tent (www.butterfly-gifts.com/live-butterfly-kits/). If you are able, start a butterfly garden, growing what butterflies need to flourish. Download a free guide with suggested plants at www.thesca.org/butterflygarden/.

Pentecost

At the end of the great fifty days of Easter we recall the moment in The Acts of the Apostles when, just as Jesus promised, the Holy Spirit comes upon the disciples like a rushing wind, like flames, giving them the power to do God's work in the world. Read the story aloud from a children's Bible or the Common English Bible. It will make you laugh. Pentecost is sometimes called the birthday of the Church, so put a candle on a cupcake. Go to church and wear red, the color of the Holy Spirit. My friend Lisa Brown lets her kids—at home and at church—color their hair with temporary red dye. Go outside and blow bubbles, fly a kite, make pinwheels, give red balloons away to strangers. The Church isn't a building; it's all of us who follow Jesus, filled with the Holy Spirit given to us in baptism, helping to bring about the kingdom of God right here, right now, in our everyday lives.

Summer Saints

The season after Pentecost is long and the color in church is green. We call it the growing season. While there are no major feasts, don't let summer keep you from celebrating. This is a perfect time to learn about some of the saints in our calendar.

Holy Women

On July 20 the Episcopal Church remembers four bold women of the nineteenth century as liberators and prophets: Elizabeth Cady Stanton, Amelia Bloomer, Sojourner Truth, and Harriet Ross Tubman. Their strong Christian identity led them to take on civil rights. As followers of Jesus, our religious lives are not separate and apart from our political or social lives.

Arguably the two most important women in the New Testament also have summer feast days: Saint Mary Magdalene, first witness of the resurrection (July 22) and Saint Mary, the mother of Jesus (August 15). Born in a time and place where women belonged to their fathers or their husbands, could not own property, could not go out alone in public, could not talk to strangers, and could not read or study the Hebrew scriptures, these two Marys challenged traditions and assumptions of the ancient world.

Jesus treated women as equals and Mary Magdalene was one of his most trusted and loved disciples. Most of what we know about her comes from the New Testament, but there are writings not included in the Bible that tell of her being a powerful leader in the early church and the one who teaches Jesus's disciples to better understand him and his message of life-changing love. One legend that is told of Mary Magdalene is that she was invited to a banquet given by the Roman Emperor Tiberius. She held an egg in her hand and told the emperor, "Christ is risen!" The Emperor laughed, and said that Jesus rising from the dead was as likely as that plain white egg she held turning red. Before he finished speaking, the egg in her hand turned deep red. Mary Magdalene then shared the news of the Resurrection with the entire court.

Mary, the mother of Jesus is, in my opinion, often misunderstood. There was nothing meek or mild about her. Greeted by the angel Gabriel, teenage Mary asserts herself and gives consent to be unmarried and pregnant, a condition punishable by stoning. Broderick Greer calls her song in the gospel of Luke, better known as the *Magnificat*, "a rebel anthem" that may have "moonlighted as Jesus's lullaby."[7]

"My soul magnifies the Lord,
    and my spirit rejoices in God my Savior,
for he has looked with favor on the lowliness of his servant.
    Surely, from now on all generations will call me blessed;
for the Mighty One has done great things for me,
    and holy is his name.
His mercy is for those who fear him
    from generation to generation.

He has shown strength with his arm;
    he has scattered the proud in the thoughts of their hearts.
He has brought down the powerful from their thrones,
    and lifted up the lowly;
he has filled the hungry with good things,
    and sent the rich away empty.
He has helped his servant Israel,
    in remembrance of his mercy,
according to the promise he made to our ancestors,
    to Abraham and to his descendants for ever."
Luke 1:47–55

If Mary—poor, uneducated, and a woman—had these subversive thoughts two thousand years ago, then maybe Jesus was every bit as much his mother's son as his Father's.

Holy Men

Of course, you don't have to limit yourselves to the women, or to those who lived long ago. During the summer the Episcopal Church also honors two men of the twentieth century whose stories may be less familiar: Albert Lutuli (July 21) who worked against apartheid in South Africa, and Jonathan Daniels (August 14), a seminarian who died protecting a sixteen-year-old civil rights activist in Alabama in 1965.

Don't feel bound by the summer months, either. Take a look at an online liturgical calendar,[8] see who's there, read their stories, be inspired.

Fall Saints

The Feast of St Francis

Among the most beloved of saints is twelfth-century Francis of Assisi. Francis was born into a wealthy Italian family. A party boy, he loved all the finer things in life and found adventure as a knight until he was captured and imprisoned for a year. Following his release (his father having paid a large ransom), he found himself in a church that was falling down and, as he prayed, Francis heard God tell him to rebuild it. He sold a bale of his father's silk to pay for the repairs, which angered his father. The bishop told Francis that God would give him what he needed, so Francis gave his father his purse of gold coins—and every stitch of clothing he was wearing.

From that time on, Francis wore only burlap and gave up all his belongings to live among and serve the poor and the sick. Francis followed Jesus in his actions, not just his words, and soon he had followers of his own who wanted to live simply and serve God and others as he did. He took special notice and care of God's creation. One of the stories told about him is that he helped a village make friends with a wolf that had been attacking their animals. Even the birds flocked around him as he told them of God's love. Francis may even have staged the first Christmas pageant, with real animals to warm the Christ child in the stable. Francis died in the same little church that he rebuilt with his own hands. He still inspires others with his generosity, his joy in God's creation, and his simple, peaceful ways.

Many churches celebrate his feast day, October 4, with a Blessing of the Animals. A great family activity is making dog biscuits and cat toys (feathers and jingle bells tied with bright yarn to a stick) to give away or to benefit a local animal shelter. You can also make a bird feeder by spreading peanut or soy butter onto the scales of a pinecone and rolling it in birdseed. Use a chenille stem to make a sturdy loop and hang it on a tree branch. Even toddlers can string Cheerios onto a chenille stem for another bird treat that's easily hung.

Martin of Tours

Martin of Tours was the son of a soldier in the Roman Army of the fourth century. He first attended church at the age of ten, against his parents' wishes. When Martin was fifteen, he was required to join the army himself and served in Amiens, France. One winter night, he saw a beggar at the city gates shivering with cold. Martin had no money to give him, but he took off his heavy cloak and sliced it in half with his sword, giving half to the beggar. That night, Jesus came to Martin in a dream, wrapped in half of Martin's cloak. Martin's biographer, who knew him personally, wrote that the next day Martin "flew to be baptized." He decided that he could not be both a soldier and a follower of Jesus. Eventually and reluctantly, he became Bishop of Tours.

The piece of cloak that Martin kept was saved and much later, French kings swore oaths on it and carried it into battle. The words *chapel* and *chaplain* both come from the French word that means "little cloak," for the small temporary churches that were used to hold the cloak and for the priest who took care of it. Eventually, all priests who served in the military caring for soldiers were called chaplains, and small churches everywhere became known as chapels.

Today he is remembered as the patron of all those who serve in the military, and the day of his death, November 11, is also Veteran's Day when we honor those who have fought for the protection of others.

In the Middle Ages, Advent began with the Feast of St. Martin and lasted for forty days until Christmas, just like Lent, the season that prepares us for Easter. In Europe, children still make lanterns on St. Martin's Day as the night comes early to carry his light and the light of Christ into the darkness. You could make jam jar lanterns. Better yet, host a coat drive. Your kids can make posters to put up around the neighborhood advertising the day and time. Then, let them take their wagons and go door-to-door (by lantern-light?) collecting gently used coats that can be given to those in need. If you need help distributing coats, try www.onewarmcoat.org.

Halloween, All Saints Day, and All Souls Day

What is this nonsense about Halloween being unchristian? True, the Celtic day of the dead, Samhain, predated Christianity and fell on October 31. Ancient practices and festivals have been adopted by the Church and made new in the light of Christ. To me this does not diminish the Christian holy days; it makes them stronger, more resonant.

Halloween

Hallow means holy and Halloween is a contraction of All Hallow's Eve, the night before All Saints Day, a major feast of the Church. On Halloween, we face our fears and laugh at them, knowing that nothing, not even death, can separate us from the love of God.

There is a brief liturgy for All Hallow's Eve in *The Book of Occasional Services* that churches seldom use but is easily adapted for home. Turn out the lights and let the room be lit by candles and Jack o' lanterns.

> *The leader begins:* Light and peace, in Jesus Christ our Lord.
> *The response is:* Thanks be to God.
> *The leader:* Be our light in the darkness, O Lord, and by your great mercy defend us from all perils and dangers of this night, for the love of your son, our savior Jesus Christ.
> *Everyone responds:* Amen.

The first reading is the story of Saul and the Witch of Endor (1 Samuel 28:3–25). You'll want to substitute "witch" for "medium" so it will be more recognizable if you are using the Common English Bible or the NRSV.

The second reading is Ezekiel in the Valley of Dry Bones (Ezekiel 37:1–14). This one would be simple to print out and divide up for two people to read the parts of God and Ezekiel. When I've done this with little ones, they like to lie on the floor and be the bones in the desert. Use a maraca for the rattling noise. What could you use for the sound of God's breath? Your bones can jump up and dance at the appropriate time in the story.

End with the Lord's Prayer. Before you go out to trick-or-treat, you could sing a song, maybe this hymn, sung to the tune of the Tallis canon:

All praise to thee, my God this night
For all the blessings of the light.
Keep me, o keep me, King of Kings
Beneath thine own almighty wings.

All Saints Day

All Saints Day is when we lift up all those who are part of the Communion of Saints. We've told the stories of many of them in this chapter, but there are so many more with equally compelling stories and legends. This is a day for baptisms in the church, and often a list of all those who have died since the last All Saints Day is read aloud. We have sometimes made a paper chain on which we've written the names of those we love who have died as a tangible reminder that we are linked with them and all who follow Jesus through baptism.

All Souls Day

November 2 is the "commemoration of all faithful departed," a day to remember our own family and friends who have died. It's a good time to visit a cemetery, which should not be a place of fear but of respect. No one minds if you make rubbings of old gravestones. The churchyard where I work has markers dating back to the late 17th century. Mexican friends observe this day with serious play and even joy as the Day of the Dead, making family altars with photographs, flowers, candles, and food. Light a candle, say a prayer, tell stories of the ones we love and see no longer.

Soon it will be Advent. We begin again. The liturgical calendar is a countercultural one. Don't let it complicate your family life—let it enrich it.

CHAPTER 6

Making Home Holy

Then my people will live in a peaceful dwelling, in secure homes, in carefree resting places. Isaiah 32:18 (CEB)

Here's the thing: for your child, home is already holy and you are the one who makes it so. You are modeling God's love and care by making your child feel safe and secure, nurtured and supported. Everything else is just window dressing. The rhythms of the day, the year, and the seasons of our lives are full of opportunities to find and create sacred moments, ways of making meaning and memories, and all of them can be simple.

Mealtime

Start tonight, with dinner. Can you all sit down together? It's okay if you are sitting down to take-out. Light candles. Hold hands around the table and let the youngest child choose when to squeeze. No cellphones, no television. Music might be nice, without lyrics. You'll find some mealtime blessings in chapter 2: Talking with God.

Setting the Table

I aspire to cloth napkins every night, but that adds to the laundry load. My father remembers that his grandfather insisted on cloth napkins for every meal. There were silver napkin rings for special occasions and wooden clothespins with people's names on them, even guests, for everyday use, so the napkins could be reused. This memory led to my family collecting napkin rings. Whoever set the table on Friday could choose the napkin rings, and we had lots of fun choices: olive wood from Jerusalem, a hand-painted folk art set from Austria, enameled ones from India. If you don't have any, your kids can twist pipe cleaners into circles. If they want to get fancy, cut a cardboard tube into pieces and let them wrap each ring in a different color ribbon, one for each member of the family.

Do you have a bit more time? Ask your kids to find an object with meaning to set on a small plate and use as a centerpiece. It could be a baseball, or a baby cup, or a postcard from Nana. Let them tell about why they chose it. You can be directive: bring something that makes you feel proud, something that reminds you of when you were tiny, or something that's beautiful.

What will you talk about tonight? Conversation cards are fun even if you never get stuck on what to ask instead of "How was school today?" Make your own. Ask questions you'd like to respond to yourself, or ones you don't know the answer to: What is your favorite memory? If you could have one superpower, what would it be? Where would you go if you could go anywhere in the world? Describe your perfect day. Tell about an act of kindness you saw today. How would you spend $100 (or $100,000) on other people? Throw in a God question, maybe not right away: When do you feel closest to God?

The Jewish tradition of the Shabbat (Sabbath) dinner on Friday nights is one from which we can learn and borrow. Rituals of the Temple were brought into Jewish homes after the destruction of the Temple in 73 CE and the family table rather than the altar became the place where God's people were reconciled to God. Laurie David, author of a great cookbook called *The Family Dinner* asserts that the Shabbat symbols are relevant today and for non-Jews as well:

> "The candlesticks, the challah and the wine all represent contemporary goals: a regularly scheduled moment to pause, to express gratitude for the food we eat, to bless our children and one another. Whatever our religion, the core truths are universal: gratitude for all that we have, compassion for those who have less, family togetherness, peace in the home, love and hope for the future."[1]

Among the many meaningful Shabbat customs (lighting candles, giving thanks for the bread and the wine, talking only of happy things) are two that you might consider adding to your special family dinners. Before everyone comes to the table, they empty their pockets of coins from the week to put in a *tzedakah* box. The Hebrew root of this word means justice, and the money that is collected is set aside for giving to a cause or an organization that you choose as a family. Another custom is that parents bless their children (and in some families, children also bless their parents). The traditional words name Biblical ancestors whose character traits are worthy of inheriting, but you may use whatever words hold meaning for your family. The idea is that the blessing given to the children encourages them to be a blessing to others. Jewish parents place a hand on their child's head and speak the blessing, although if that seems too formal, you could take your child's hands in yours. This honors the bond that connects us from those who have been examples of how to live in faith, to those whose lives we touch.

Holidays Meals

Holidays (and the meals that are often part of them) hold extra joy. The holidays of my childhood that shine so brightly in my memory were spent at my grandparents' home, where everyone around the table was family, every dish was delicious, and while I know it's not true that no one ever argued, what I remember is how much love I felt.

For most of my adult life I have lived far from my family. However, holidays have been no less joyful. Now we most often spend Christmas Day and Easter Day with our friends

Kathy and Greg, whose table seems to grow larger every year. Kathy says she inherited this tradition from her mother, Eileen. "We never lived near family as my dad was a military officer and my mom is from England. So our family was the neighborhood, military base, or community we lived in. My mom had an open door policy and invited neighbors, friends and most especially anyone who didn't have a place to go." Greg recalls that after college, when his immediate family had moved away from the Northeast, he was taken in, "given a place at the table" for holiday meals and "made to feel like family. It gave me a deep appreciation for there being people who don't have family close by and face experiencing 'gathering' events on their own. What's the price of a bit more food or a tighter squeeze around the table compared with the warmth and joy an open door can bring?"

Guests are invited to bring a favorite dish, but of course no one has to bring a thing. Kathy, who is a wonderful cook, says, "The food is important, but in the end it's about who is gathered at our table and that they come and join us. I always think that the absolute best gift is someone's presence."

Family Stories

Family dinners are important, but not because it's dinner. Sitting down together over any meal, talking about our day, our lives—that's what makes a difference. Martin Luther King Sr. was a pastor who made a point of serious conversation around the dinner table, telling his young children about the injustices he encountered as a black man in the South in the 1930s and '40s, and how he confronted it. Years later, his daughter wrote, "These stories were as nourishing as the food that was set before us."[2] We can imagine how these stories inspired his son. There needs to be a place where we tell each other the things that are on our hearts, the stories that really matter, whether they are from that day's news or from the classroom, office, or playground. Where everyone is gathered and candles warm the room, truths can be safely shared.

Most children enjoy hearing family stories—when their parents were younger, or their grandparents. Bring out the photo albums (do people still make photo albums?) and remember people, pets, and places. They also love hearing stories about their younger selves. Knowing family stories provides a sense of connectedness and identity. Research over the last thirty years has demonstrated that children who know their family histories benefit in a variety of significant ways, among them the ability to find themselves in a larger narrative—what researchers Marshall Duke and Robyn Fivush call a strong "intergenerational self."[3] Stories of how families have overcome hardships are especially important in helping children and teens develop resilience, self-confidence and self-esteem.[4]

Let me add, in case it's not perfectly obvious, that one of the reasons we tell Bible stories is to connect ourselves to something larger. As my friend Episcopal priest Kerlin Richter says, "The Bible keeps me tethered to a people and a story that have been there long before me and a story that will be here long after me."[5] Pastor Jodi Houge puts it more simply: "It's another storyline that tells me I'm beloved."[6]

Birthdays

The celebration of a birthday or anniversary is always special, of course. Develop a tradition or two of your own for your family, or continue one that you remember from your childhood. Find photos of the birthday child or adult through the years; put them in frames placed all around the house, make a collage of them on a bulletin board or the refrigerator.

The Book of Common Prayer has a birthday blessing (two, in fact) that can be prayed at breakfast, with everyone placing their hand on the birthday person:

Look with favor, we pray, on your servant (name here) as s/he begins another year. Grant that s/he may grow in wisdom and grace, and strengthen her/his trust in your goodness all the days of her/his life; through Jesus Christ our Lord. Amen.[7]

Some families invite everyone to take turns giving compliments to the birthday person, but another tradition I really like is that each family member and guest makes a special wish aloud for the birthday person before the candles are blown out. We have a different birthday song—one that I learned from a family at church years ago, subtly different from the classic. It's sung to the tune of "The Merry Widow Waltz":

Happy birthday, happy birthday, we love you.
Happy birthday, and may all your dreams come true.
When you blow out the candles, one light stays aglow:
It's the love-light in your eyes where e'er you go.

For us it's a lovely reminder that every candle symbolizes the light of Christ, the spark of God that shines in each one of us.

Until we moved from California when Peter was five-and-a-half, he didn't know that children brought gifts to birthday parties. (The first birthday party he attended in Connecticut came as a shock to him, let me tell you.) We were part of a parents' group in California that agreed our kids didn't need more things, so instead of exchanging gifts we exchanged books. We requested dinosaur books for the dinosaur-themed party when Peter was three. Everyone took home a book, including Peter, and so it was for every birthday with this set of friends.

Many children can be overwhelmed by the gifts and the focus on themselves. I have a friend who just turned fifty and celebrated with fifty acts of kindness and generosity she gave to strangers and those in need. What if we honored our children's years that way, and invited them to take part in giving? One year Peter invited friends and family members to purchase mosquito nets for families in Africa through Episcopal Relief and Development as a way of helping him celebrate his birthday. The animal-loving daughter of my friend Pamela asked her friends to shop for pets instead of for her and the gifts were given to a local animal shelter as part of the celebration. My friend Day began giving her daughters gifts of donations to worthy causes they were interested in when they entered high school, wrapping the certificates for them to open. This year on Mother's Day she received something similar from her youngest daugh-

ter: the gift of prenatal care to a mother in need. "Needless
to say," Day told me, "it was the best gift ever."

Adoption Days

Families who have adopted children celebrate more than
birthdays. They honor in a variety of ways how their child
came to be theirs. Sheryl Kujawa-Holbrook told me, "We
celebrate our daughter's 'Gotcha Day' with Guatema-
lan stories and food. Other days that are celebrated are
the final court date. For adoption children who can grow
uncertain about their belonging—why was I given up?—it
can be helpful to feel 'chosen.' There is also a rite of passage in the adoption world, where parents bring their child
to the country or city of their birth—around ages eleven
to thirteen."

My friend MaryAlice, whose daughters were adopted in
Russia, lived in Kazakhstan for three years and because of
that, "our home has many Central Asian elements like rugs
and paintings; I cook Russian every now and then. . . . but
not on a specific day." On Mother's Day, her daughters know
that MaryAlice's prayers are with their birth mother, that she
is at peace wherever she may be. "I do take it as sacred duty
to honor my daughters' early loss and it's my honor to walk
alongside them."

Another family I know celebrates the day their son's
adoption was finalized with a family gathering—Grandma
bakes a cake, or sweet potato pie. I remember well that first
adoption day, because as the children's minister of MJ's

church, I was invited to their home to pray with them. We used this, from *Thanksgiving for a Child* in the Book of Common Prayer (p. 443):

O God, you have taught us through your blessed son that whoever receives a little child in the name of Christ receives Christ himself: We give you thanks for the blessing you have bestowed upon (this family) in giving them a child. Confirm their joy by a lively sense of your presence with them, and give them calm strength and patient wisdom as they seek to bring this child to love all that is true and noble, just and pure, lovable and gracious, excellent and admirable, following the example of our Lord and Savior, Jesus Christ. Amen.

"There are so many adoptive families out there and a new person shares their story in random places I go, at the grocery store, the gym, the park. It's holy in those moments too," MJ notes.

Anniversaries

Wedding anniversaries are often something adults celebrate without including their kids, but even if you go to dinner without them you can share a special memory of that day, read them one of the passages from scripture that was read at your wedding and tell them why you chose it, and have the traditional wedding dessert: cake.

What about baptismal anniversaries? Invite your child's godparents to dinner or call them on the phone. Skype is even better if they can't be there in person. They can help tell the story of your child's baptism. Find the baptism candle, or any white candle, light it and set it next to an empty bowl. Your child can pour water into the bowl from a pitcher. I wrote this prayer for my young friends Madeleine and Frances.

Tonight we remember the baptism of (your child's name here). You were baptized with water in the name of the Father and of the Son and of the Holy Spirit, and you were marked with the sign of the cross as Christ's own forever. You were given a candle as a sign that Jesus is the light of the world. In baptism we hear the voice of God saying to each of us, "You are my beloved child. I am so happy with you." May we remember that we belong to God forever, may we share the light of Christ with everyone we meet, and may we walk in love now and with the saints and angels and all the company of heaven in the life to come. Amen.

Family Nights

What happens after dinner, even one night a week? Do you play board games? What about a dance party? An evening walk? The goal here is something that brings all of you together. When Peter was small, he loved to make pillow forts, inside in cold weather or rainy days and outside on a quilt in warm weather. It was the perfect spot to read bedtime stories and say our prayers. A particular treat was to have dessert (or breakfast the next morning) squeezed inside the cozy fort.

Let's say you have a family movie night, or choose chapter books to read aloud. Please know that you do not have to watch or read anything overtly religious in order to find God in them. Aran Walter invites the kids and parents he works with to learn to use a "Kingdom of God" filter:

"Whether its film or music or something else, once you strip away the Hollywood and you start to have conversations about it, you're going to end up looking into what God is doing in the world and how we can direct our lives towards what God is doing."[8]

Your kids are likely to be better at this than you are, but given some time and practice, you'll catch on. Another way to deepen the shared experience of a book or movie is to add another chapter or an alternate ending, or come up with a sequel of your family's own devising.

Books are better than television or digital screens the closer one gets to bedtime, and the practice of reading aloud doesn't need to stop when your kids reach a certain age. One dad and daughter kept up a reading streak for nine years that ended only when she left for college. Even the night of Alice's prom was a reading night with Dad. "Before I went out, I had my hair in my up-do and my fancy dress on," she recalls. "And I just sort of climbed into the bed next to him and he read to me. That's what had to happen."[9] Alice has since written a book about the streak called *The Reading Promise*, with suggestions for starting one of your own. Alice's dad Jim sees the collection of books they've read from and the streak itself as a legacy. "I don't have much money to pass on," he said. "But these books, she'll read to hers and they'll read to theirs. And they'll read to the generations down the lines. It's a means for me to touch generations I'll never see."[10]

Crossing Thresholds

Bedtime

Bedtime is the first threshold experience we remember. We close our eyes and prepare to enter another world vastly different from the one we live in during our waking hours. No wonder kids (and some adults) often have such a hard time with it. Letting go of the day and getting ready to sleep is important for the health and well-being of people of all ages.

How do we make a bedtime routine calming and soothing? Begin with a bath. A drop or two of essential oil such as lavender is enough. My friend Brook Packard says, "Some children respond well to calm, peaceful touching. You can use almond, coconut, or jojoba oil, gently massaging feet, or the back of the neck, or even the child's hands. There is an acupressure point on your child's forehead, just above the eyebrows, that when stroked for half a minute, will calm your child down."[11]

Brook has also created downloadable "bedtime kits" for families, with lullabies, a bedtime story and poems, and a mindfulness meditation to "put the day to bed." Peter has long had trouble falling asleep and uses a technique that my husband Phil taught him from his own practice of centering prayer, using the imagery of letting thoughts float down a stream, as Brook does in one of her meditations, which reminds me of a poetic *Examen* (found on page 16):

> "With your eyes closed, see that you are standing
> in tall yellow grass near a gentle stream.
> The stream bubbles along, over pebbles and stones.

You look around and see a long twig with several
   branches on it.
You pick up the twig and swirl it in the water.
The water of the stream flows around the twig.
Now think back on your day. . . ."[12]

And at each prompt, the child in her imagination breaks
off a piece of the twig and lets it float down the stream along
with the pleasures and distractions of the day. Bedtime is
holy, if we can get there with a measure of peace. You will
find a section on bedtime prayers and Compline in chapter
2: Talking with God.

It doesn't always start off that way, but invariably, in those
moments in the dark beside Peter's bed, no matter how
exasperated I have been minutes before about unfinished
homework and the length of his shower (which seems to be
inversely proportional to the length of time he should have
been studying), when we finally pray together, we let go of
our tensions with each other, too. The order for Compline,
our church's tradition of bedtime prayers, begins with the
words, "The Lord Almighty grant us a peaceful night and a
perfect end." We may not get our perfect end on a daily basis,
but a peaceful night makes all the difference.

Going Out and Coming In

Sharon Pearson tells me that above the front door inside the
house where she grew up, her parents hung a small cross
that says, "Bless those who come in and out." It wasn't something they talked about, but it was always there, and now
it hangs above the door in the home she shares with her
family. My friend Katherine gets up before her children to

pray for them. When they come downstairs they can smell the scented candle she lights as she begins, and they know exactly what that means.

Even though Peter is old enough to pack his own lunch, I continue to pack his not only because he likes it, but because I remember the school lunches my mother packed for me as being special, a sign of her love which I took with me. They often included handwritten notes, jokes, or riddles and decorated napkins left over from a special occasion. Now that Peter is older, his lunches sometimes include a treat to share with friends. Some families have secret handshakes. I know a mom who gives her kids lipstick kisses, and when they get too big for ones on the cheek, she presses her lips to a piece of paper to be tucked in a pocket. When I occasionally took trips without Peter, he made sure I had a small stuffed animal in my suitcase to keep me company. My husband, who travels for work twice a month, has noticed that we cheer (softly, so as not to disturb the neighbors) when he comes home. These are little things, but they count. God is in our comings and goings.

House Blessings

Moving is hard in so many ways. Saying goodbye to your home and your neighborhood can make the transition easier. One family, who lived in their home twelve years, went on a tour of their empty house, "telling stories in every room and then blessing the room with thanks to God for all that had happened there."[13] The goodbye party ended with ice cream. When the family moved to their new house, they went from room to room in a similar fashion. *Of course* they went out to their new favorite place for ice cream afterward.

When my friend Anna moved, she and her family made a time capsule to bury in the front lawn. In it went pictures drawn by her kids, photographs including one of the whole family, and a Bible verse. When it comes time to move again one day, they'll dig it up and remember their childhood.

There's an iconic scene in the movie *It's a Wonderful Life*, when Mary and George Bailey, standing on the threshold of their new neighbors' home, offer three symbolic gifts:

> *Mary Bailey:* Bread so that this house may never know hunger. Salt so that life may always have flavor.
> *George Bailey:* Wine that joy and prosperity may reign forever.

Ree Drummond, better known as The Pioneer Woman, says that the blessing "reflects a sentiment woven throughout the story, that things of true worth are not measured in dollars, but in the currency of friendship and family, and the good karma one puts out into the world. Maybe best expressed by the motto in Peter Bailey's office: 'All you can take with you is that which you've given away.'"[14]

There are more religious ways of blessing a house, and your priest or minister would very likely be happy to do so, but designing one as a family can be a meaningful way to begin life in your new home.

Welcoming a New Baby

When my brother Gregg was born I was almost three. I thought he was my baby, that the only reason my parents were having a baby was for me. My sister Amy was born to my father and stepmother when I was eighteen—actually perfect timing, since I could practice mothering without any consequences. Not all siblings react this way, I'm told. When my friend Anna gives birth to her fourth child this year, she will ask her older children to bring something of their own that they'd like to share with the baby when they meet her, something that will help the baby "know" how special her siblings are.

Peter is an only child, and my favorite gift was a "baby blessings" book filled with messages from people who had attended the baby shower, visited us in the hospital, come to our home in those early days bearing meals, or attended his baptism. To this day I can't read it without getting teary.

There is a sweet Thanksgiving for the Birth or Adoption of a Child in the Book of Common Prayer (439–445) that can be used in the hospital or at church, at home or in the courthouse. One of the prayers can be found in the Adoption section above.

School Days

School is so strongly tied to home life for so many years that it's worth mentioning some rituals to consider. Several years ago I wrote a backpack blessing that has made its way through the Episcopal Church and beyond. Last year it appeared on a Sunday bulletin insert at my mother's church in California! On the first day of school, tuck a small cross or angel token into the pocket of your children's backpacks and use these words:

God of Wisdom, we give you thanks for schools and class-rooms and for the teachers and students who fill them each day. We thank you for this new beginning, for new books and new ideas. We thank you for sharpened pencils, pointy cray-ons, and crisp blank pages waiting to be filled. We thank you for the gift of making mistakes and trying again. Help us to remember that asking the right questions is often as impor-tant as giving the right answers. Today we give you thanks for these your children, and we ask you to bless them with curiosity, understanding and respect. May their backpacks be a sign to them that they have everything they need to learn and grow this year in school and in Sunday School. May they be guided by your love. All this we ask in the name of Jesus, who as a child in the temple showed his longing to learn about you, and as an adult taught by story and example your great love for us. Amen.

On the sidewalk outside our Brooklyn apartment I have seen colorful chalked messages of encouragement from par-ents to children on the first day of school: "Have fun!" "Make new friends!" "Listen well!"

Homework will be a thing no matter what. My advice is to make it as painless as possible for everyone. A healthy snack beforehand helps, as does a short break between get-ting home and starting the work. Having a place to study is ideal; in our home it's the kitchen table. I often pray for it to go quickly, but that's a silent prayer, for my own sanity. I practice patience and try to ask helpful questions, including "How much homework do you have?" and "What do you need from me?" I know my child well enough to know that he always underestimates the time it will take to complete an assignment, so sometimes setting a timer for fifteen minutes of concentrated effort is more successful than giving him half an hour when he'll spend part of that time daydreaming.

I am fortunate to have a kid who loves school, and we take special care each year to make sure his teachers know how grateful we are for all they've done, usually with gifts of homemade cookies. My friend Kathy goes a step further with her kids: they write thank-you notes to each teacher at the end of every school year. Now that they are in high school, this takes greater effort, but I can't help thinking of the students' notes I have kept and treasured from my teaching days a million years ago.

When a Pet Dies

The death of a pet is often our children's first experience of death. Yes, I have flushed dead goldfish down the toilet, but learn from my mistake: there are better ways to handle it. Frank Logue, an Episcopal priest, has created a liturgy for families to use that will help give shape and some appropriate gravitas to a pet funeral,[15] though you should also feel free to let your kids design and lead this. At the very least, they may want to give a brief eulogy, telling those assembled what they loved and will miss about their pet. Judith Viorst's classic picture book, *The Tenth Good Thing About Barney*, is a must-read in this situation.

For a fuller discussion about death and children, please see chapter 7: Finding God in Difficult Times.

Milestones

You might not have realized how many family traditions you already have until you read this chapter. Meg Cox, author of *The Book of New Family Traditions* prefers the word "ritual" because it "covers more ground. It's a stretchy word that covers everything from saying grace to big ceremonies like weddings and funerals."[16] (This book, by the way, is well worth having on your shelf, covering as it does a wide array of creative, meaningful, and fun rituals for holidays and everyday life.)

Rituals are found in every human culture; they are how we impart values and a sense of family, religious, and ethnic identity. Rituals both mark and make transitions, and they are beneficial in helping us cope in times of difficulty and loss. The Church recognizes this. Amazingly, there is an official publication of the Episcopal Church called *Changes: Prayers and Services Honoring Rites of Passage* that covers a vast array of such occasions, including moving from a crib to a bed, becoming a reader, going away to camp, reaching puberty (God help us), earning a driver's license, and going to college. There are prayers for midlife: ending a job, surviving a tragedy, healing after divorce, and taking on the care of elder parents. There are also prayers for elders (becoming a grandparent, celebrating significant birthdays or anniversaries), prayers for national service, and prayers for remembering those who have died. *How* your family marks occasions like these is far less important than *that* your family marks them in some way.

Blessing Bowls

One way to mark milestones as well as to prompt meaningful conversations is to have a "blessing bowl." Milestones Ministries[17] sells one that comes with a set of hand-painted ceramic stones with particular assigned meanings. They suggest a number of times and ways to use them, such as, "at a family gathering, invite each person to pick a stone and share a recent milestone experience," or, "carry a stone in your pocket as a reminder of the people and the God whose love goes with you," or, "pass the blessing bowl at the dinner table and have every family member share a story of his or her day." You can also order additional stones for special events, like one with a car key painted on it for getting a driver's license, and ones to mark graduations from middle school, high school, and college.

You could make something like this yourself. Choose any bowl you really like, although a shallow one will display the items you choose to put in it well. Then, collect some small items to put in it. We have just started one of our own, using a small beautiful bowl painted gold on the inside that was a wedding present from Peter's godparents. The tiny treasures inside the bowl are meant to spark meaningful conversation, prayers, remembrances, and gratitude. Here is what we have found so far:

- a marble painted like the earth, for travel, for those we love who are far from us, for being mindful of world events
- a blue jay feather, for journeys (school trips, camp, vacations)
- a heart-shaped stone, for acts of love and generosity
- an acorn, for growth
- an angel token, for acts of caring and kindness
- a LEGO piece, for play, fun, and creativity
- a silk rainbow ribbon for promises made and kept
- a pottery pebble that says "peace", for when we find it or when we need it
- a small olivewood cross, to notice where Jesus has been with us that day

The rainbow ribbon was what we held up last night, to honor the significant commitment Peter made in writing and delivering a sermon at our dinner church, St. Lydia's. I've kept the peace pebble close at hand on stressful days as a literal touchstone. The world marble is always a connection to Phors, who lives in Cambodia, part of our extended family since he and Peter were both five through a World Vision sponsorship.

"We don't remember days, we remember moments," says the Italian poet Cesare Pavese.[18] Parents know this best. The warmth and love we create in our families may not be something that feels consistently present, but it is what we hope our children carry with them and learn to create for themselves and others. These moments of sacred connection can sustain us for a lifetime.

CHAPTER 7

Finding God in Difficult Times

✝

For I am convinced that neither death, nor life, nor angels, nor rulers, nor things present, nor things to come, nor powers, nor height, nor depth, nor anything else in all creation, will be able to separate us from the love of God in Christ Jesus our Lord. Romans 8:38–39

Just because I don't believe in an interventionist God doesn't mean that some days I wouldn't like to. I don't really see how it would work, though. To imagine that God who is Love picks and chooses who lives and who dies doesn't make any kind of sense to me.

Where is God when terrible things happen? Why does God allow tragedy? These are questions we have asked since the beginning of time. It may not surprise you that the oldest book in the Bible, Job, takes on the problem of human suffering and how people of faith should understand it without answering the question well at all.

The idea that God intervenes in human affairs and natural disasters—or worse, chooses not to—has always been troubling to me. My understanding of God is a loving presence with us in every moment, good and terrible. As Christians, we know in Jesus a God who suffers with us, a compassionate God who understands human grief and suffering because he has grieved and suffered, too. Harold Kushner says, "God, who neither causes nor prevents tragedies, helps by inspiring people to help. As a nineteenth century Hasidic rabbi once put it, 'human beings are God's language.'"[1] Television icon and Presbyterian minister Fred Rogers is still widely quoted when tragedy strikes:

> "When I was a boy and I would see scary things in the news, my mother would say to me, 'Look for the helpers. You will always find people who are helping.' To this day, especially in times of 'disaster,' I remember my mother's words and I am always comforted by realizing that there are still so many helpers—so many caring people in this world."[2]

This is how God acts in times of trouble, in and through us.

On September 16, 2001, I walked back after lunch to the church where I had begun work only the month before, on the Upper East Side of New York City. As I came through the front door and my eyes adjusted to the dim light, I could see two people sitting in the front pew of the otherwise empty sanctuary: a woman and a young girl. I grabbed a few blank index cards and a fistful of crayons from a basket, walked over and knelt down beside them. I introduced myself and handed the child the crayons and index cards. "This is Annie, and I'm her aunt," the woman told me. "Annie's father died on Tuesday, and she is wondering who is keeping her safe now." I took a deep breath, said a silent prayer, and began.

"Well, Annie, your mother and your aunts and uncles are keeping you safe. So are the firefighters, and the police officers, the mayor and the president." I paused, and pointed to the paschal candle in front of us, which had been lit and placed in the center of the chancel as soon as we heard the news of the second plane hitting the towers. "Do you see this candle? We sometimes call it the Christ candle, and it's there to remind us that God's love is stronger than anything, even death. Jesus is here with us, and we are safe in God's love." I don't remember if I said anything else. What I will never forget is that Annie drew three pictures. The first was of the paschal candle, the second was of the dark church with jewel-bright stained glass windows, and the third was the sun blazing in the sky. Annie *knew*. I simply reminded her.

Death as Part of Life

Tragedy is always difficult and the death of those we love is always painful, but it's only in the last few generations that we have been increasingly removed from death as a part of life. More people grew up on farms and saw the life cycle of crops and animals; grandparents lived in the same home as their grandchildren; people became ill and died at home rather than in hospitals. We have made death something to fear and to hide from instead of recognizing it as the natural end of all living things, and I think our children have not been well served in this. I have friends who have gone to great lengths to protect their children from even the death of a pet, replacing an identical fish before the child has noticed and grieved.

We also should be wary of letting the media (including video games) be what our children know of death. Death should not be trivialized, but it can be normalized. It's up to us to model this for our kids.

How to Help Children in Difficult Times:

- Comfort them, assure them, *be* with them.
- Tell them that it's okay to feel whatever it is that they are feeling. Help them name what they are feeling. Tell them what you are feeling, too, and don't be afraid to show your emotions.
- Make sure they understand nothing that has happened is their fault.
- Tell them what they need to know as clearly and simply as you can. The facts surrounding traumatic events are far better coming from you than from any other source.
- Don't use euphemisms. Say died, not "passed away." Equating death with sleep or a long trip is a really bad idea. Even saying "God needed another angel" or "God has taken them to heaven" is problematic,

because children may fear that God will want to take them, too.

• Limit their exposure to the news (if it is a local or national tragedy) and/or adult conversation.

• Listen to their questions. What they are actually asking is not necessarily what we think they are asking. My case in point is Peter at three: When he began to understand in a different way that he had just one parent, he started asking about what would happen to him if I died. I kept reassuring him. He was frustrated. One morning as I was unbuckling him from the car seat in the preschool drop-off lane, he said to me, "If you die today or tomorrow, who will drive this car and take me where I need to go?" What Peter needed to know was that I had a plan for him.

• You are allowed to say that you don't know or that you don't understand either. It's healthy and helpful to let your children know that you don't have all the answers.

In the event of a tragedy, by all means tell your children that this (natural disaster, school shooting, death of a child) is very rare, and that God did not cause it—or any other death, illness, accident—to happen.

There are a number of excellent resources available as you make your way through a time of crisis. *When Bad Things Happen to Good People* by Harold Kushner deserves its status as a classic in the field. He writes for adults clearly and with compassion from his experience as a rabbi and a parent. *Talking About Death: A Dialogue Between Parent and Child* by Earl Grollman is also still relevant and very helpful, although there is no religious framing. New this year is a children's book, *Death is Stupid* by Anastasia Higgenbottham, which is refreshingly honest and sensitive, while leaving room for your own beliefs. Artist and writer Roger Hutchison's book, *The Painting Table: A Journal of Loss and Joy* is a gentle and creative way for a family to reflect together on grief and loss.

Helping Others in the Midst of Their Grief

Show up. Please, please show up. So many of us back away; we are afraid to come close, as if cancer or the death of a spouse or a child is somehow contagious. You may not know what to say. Say that. Say, "I have no words." It's fine to sit in silence, to hold your friend as she cries, to cry with her. The real ministry is being present.

Do not say, "Please let me know if I can help." Be specific. Call from the grocery store and say, "I am picking up dinner for you. Would you like me to choose, or do you have some suggestions?" Say, "I'm coming over to do your laundry," or offer to pick up their kids from school and spend the afternoon with them. People in crisis have practical needs and you can *do* something. Can you go to doctor's appointments with them? That can be of tremendous value. In fact, you can learn how to clean a feeding tube and administer morphine. You may not think you can, but trust me on this. What your friend is doing is so much harder.

Be aware of how you speak of God. It is never God's will or God's plan for a loved one to be ill or to die. Equally unhelpful is "God never gives you more than you can handle," because God simply doesn't work like that. Even "he's in a better place" is hurtful, because no matter what heaven is like, when someone loses a spouse or a child, there is no better place that person could be than with their family. When I found myself spending time with a family who had recently learned their youngest child was dying, a wise priest who had also been a hospice chaplain told me, "In much of this, God will feel more present to you than to them." That made me think about what I was doing in a different way: I wasn't there to bring them God; I found God when I was with them, sipping tea or emptying the dishwasher or sitting at the bedside of their sweet and beloved child. It is a sacred thing, to come close to people in this time, but the gift will be yours to receive.

Don't shield your own children. Let them make cards, help prepare a meal, visit. Let them see how we take care of each other in times of need.

Funerals

Children can and should go to funerals if they want to go. Methodist minister Melissa Florer-Bixler writes,

> Funerals make space within the church, among God's people, for children to explore the strangeness of life's end. It is here that they see adults vulnerable to grief; that they sense the magnitude of what we face. Here children also learn that we carry this grief together. It is at funerals that we discover that, even in the end, there is nowhere we can

go from God's love—because we see it in the people gathered around us.[3]

Christian funerals in the liturgical churches are framed as celebrations of life. The color of the altar covering and the vestments worn by the clergy is white because we are Easter people; we know that death is not the end of this story either, even if we aren't exactly clear on the details of what happens next. The liturgy itself helps us embrace the mystery.

Those who have died live on in our memories. Tell their stories, talk about them, show photos, listen to their favorite music, and visit the places that were special to them. I have "memories" of my great-grandmothers whom I never met, because my parents and grandparents have shared their stories with such warmth and vividness. Our loved ones are still present in the love we share with each other.

What About Heaven?

Please talk to your children about heaven if it brings you comfort; and even if you are unsure about it, imagining what it might be like can be a helpful tool for them. There are some lovely picture books that can give you a way in. A dear friend used *Dog Heaven* by Cynthia Rylant with her children to talk with them, not about the death of a pet, but of a loved one and found that the remove of dogs from people meant that she could get through it and the resulting conversation without crying. If heaven is so wonderful for the dogs in this book, how much more wonderful will being with God be for the people we love? A particularly moving picture book to use with school-aged children is *The Next Place* by Warren Hanson.

When I talk about heaven, I am usually imagining the *parousia*, a Greek word that means "presence," the time at the end of time when God will be "all in all." I use this image from Revelation 21:

Look! God's dwelling is here with humankind. God will dwell with them, and they will be God's peoples . . . God will wipe away every tear from their eyes. Death will be no more. There will be no mourning, crying, or pain anymore, for the former things have passed away. (CEB)

I don't know what happens after we die, but this I believe.

Death touches all of us. If you haven't had to talk to your children about it yet, it's only a matter of time. Take heart. "Here is the world," says theologian Frederick Buechner, echoing God, "beautiful and terrible things will happen. Don't be afraid."[4] We are not afraid because we know God is with us always, and nothing, not even death, can separate us from God's love.

CHAPTER 8

Meeting God in Others

✝

Just then a lawyer stood up to test Jesus. "Teacher," he said, "what must I do to inherit eternal life?" Jesus said to him, "What is written in the law? What do you read there?" He answered, "You shall love the Lord your God with all your heart, and with all your soul, and with all your strength, and with all your mind; and your neighbor as yourself." And he said to him, "You have given the right answer; do this, and you will live." But wanting to justify himself, he asked Jesus, "And who is my neighbor?"

Luke 10:25–29

When Peter was eight months old, we moved across the country from New York City to Newport Beach, California. By the time he was nine the two of us had moved five more times. The question, "Who is my neighbor?" has been a constant for us. The first neighbors Peter remembers lived a few doors down from us in our apartment complex in South Pasadena. We met James, then ten, at the pool the week we moved in. James, his Japanese grandmother Teiko, and his mother Lisa all but adopted Peter. Then eighteen months old, Peter basked in the love and attention they gave to him, not to mention the constant supply of goldfish crackers and Hot Wheels cars. Their home was an extension of our own. When James was twelve, he was baptized and I became his godmother. The line between friends and family is often blurry in my experience.

Family and Friends

Our church was also an extension of our home: it was where I worked, where Peter went to daycare, and where we worshipped. A particularly wonderful part of my job was facilitating a weekly parents' group. The reality was that this circle of parents held me up and kept us close. My first year with them was the year that Peter's father died suddenly. I quickly discovered that I was not, in fact, raising my child alone. I was raising him in a loving, supportive community, surrounded by people with whom I shared common values, recipes and holidays, hand-me-downs and hospital visits. Occasional visits and social media have proven that the bond is still strong even across three thousand miles and twelve years.

We moved from California to Connecticut when Peter was five, the week before school started. Our upstairs neighbors, priests at the church where I would be working whom we had not yet met, had dinner waiting for us and filled our refrigerator with groceries so that I wouldn't have to go out and shop until we had settled in. On the quarter-mile walk to school we met ninety-year-old Bob, a veteran of World War II, and his Yorkshire terrier, Levi, and made a habit of stopping to chat with them each day. Bob came to see Peter march in his school's United Nations parade each year, and also the ceremony when Peter was made school ambassador. Whenever we made cookies, we brought some to Bob; he gave us tomatoes and cucumbers in the summer from his container garden; and one winter he gave Peter the Greek fisherman's cap from his coat rack that Peter still wears.

The hardest part of moving to Connecticut was the loss of our extended family and the extraordinary community at All Saints Pasadena. Dinnertime and holidays are especially lonely for a family of two, so we worked to change that. In Greenwich we had a backyard big enough for the entire kindergarten class and their families to come for a picnic, and they did. There was room at the table for nine college students and their chaplain on a choir tour from England. We celebrated Easter with friends from Mexico. One Thanksgiving we hosted a friend from Korea, a friend from Long Island, my mother from California, my uncle and his family from Atlanta, my cousin's family by marriage from Vermont, and the families of two of Peter's closest friends from school. Frequently, Karla, another single parent, and her son Grayson, Peter's best friend, brought dinner over, or we went to a diner. Sharing the meal was the important part, not whether it was homemade.

We thought we'd miss this when we moved to a tiny Brooklyn apartment, and then six months in, we discovered St. Lydia's Dinner Church. It wasn't that we needed more church in our lives, it was that we needed more people in our lives, people with whom we could sit and eat. You get to know people at a different level around the table, especially when they are not people you yourself invited. This is how strangers become friends. I met my husband at Dinner Church. Emily Scott, the pastor of St. Lydia's, says that in the breaking of the bread something happens: we catch a glimpse of Jesus in the stranger next to us at the table. "In that moment, heaven and earth overlap and God builds a bridge between the world as it is and the world as it should be."[1]

Who Is My Neighbor?

The scripture passage at the start of this chapter is the conversation that prompts Jesus to tell the parable of the Good Samaritan. A man, a Jew, is walking from Jerusalem to Jericho when he is set upon by robbers and left for dead. The religious leaders of the man's own tribe who see him by the side of the road on their way to work or worship avoid him and do not stop. The person who helps him, who carries him to safety, bandages his wounds, and pays for his care is the enemy of the Jews, the one who is *not* like him, the one Jesus's listeners would have been most surprised to hear named as the rescuer. Jesus's point was that our commonalities do not make us neighbors. Showing compassion makes us neighbors.

Our neighbors have been the women who are shelter guests at Crossroads Community Services.[2] During the day, most of these women are busy learning skills that will prepare them to transition out of homelessness. At night, they come to Crossroads for a meal and a place to sleep where it is safe, warm, and sheltered. As with so many programs, this one relies on volunteers. When we volunteer, we don't actually do much. We chat over dinner and spend the night in a room nearby. The women leave very early the next day because the church also hosts a breakfast program in the same space. Those few mornings I hope we are more aware of our own privilege, more aware of how little it takes to be a good neighbor.

Expanding our children's circles of concern from family and close friends to others whose lives and experiences may be very different from their own is a key element of developing empathy, according to researchers. A recent study—part of the "Making Caring Common" project of the Harvard Graduate School of Education—involving 10,000 youth ages twelve to eighteen, found that 80% of respondents valued personal happiness and success over caring for others.[3] Empathy is defined as the ability to "walk in someone else's shoes," but it is more than that: it is valuing *and* responding with compassion to other people and perspectives.[4] Giving our children the opportunity to know, listen to, and actively help others is essential, not only to our Christian identity and formation but to changing the society in which we live, or as Ed Bacon, the recently retired rector of All Saints Pasadena, likes to say, "turning the human race into the human family."

Wondering how to start? Writer and activist Glennon Doyle Melton wrote a letter to her son the day he began third grade. In it she tells him about a boy in her own third grade class, whom her classmates teased and she ignored, and the regret she feels about that every day. "I think that God puts people in our lives as gifts to us," Glennon tells her son. "The children in your class this year, they are some of God's gifts to you. So please treat each one like a gift from God. Every single one." She gives her son some concrete examples of how to be compassionate to his friends, like making room at the lunch table for someone eating alone, or choosing someone first for the team who is usually chosen last. That sounds like Jesus to my ears. Glennon also tells her son about his teachers and classmates, "You *Belong to Each Other*."[5] I'm pretty sure God says that, too.

Other Religions

Our upstairs neighbor Hoora spent the morning of her birthday translating a baptism class I was teaching into Farsi for a family who recently emigrated from Iran. Her husband later told me she spent hours in preparation, reading about baptism and watching videos on the Internet. I wish I knew as much about Islam as she knows now about Christianity; the best way I can think of to honor her gift of time and effort is to learn more about her beliefs and culture.

My sister's husband is Hindu, and we have been learning about his religion to better understand the traditions that my niece and nephew are growing up with. A dear friend who converted to Buddhism and is now a monk shares with us teachings and practices that she thinks will resonate in our lives. Throughout the years so many Jewish friends have welcomed us into their homes for Rosh Hashanah, Hanukkah, and Passover. I have had the privilege of both working in an interfaith center and teaching children's interfaith classes. I cannot overstate how important I think it is for all of us to better understand each other's religions, our common values as well as our differences. Yes, it is important that we articulate our own faith to our children, but in this global age, we are connected as never before, and cultivating respect for one another is essential to the health and well-being of everyone who calls this planet home.

Once, we met an Israeli engineer on a flight from New York City to North Carolina and much to his surprise, Peter sang him the *Shema* in Hebrew: "Hear, O Israel: the Lord is our God, the Lord is One."[6] We are, each of us, made in the image of God and when we look for God in everyone we meet, we are reminded of what and who makes us one.

At every baptism, Peter has heard this vow and last May at his confirmation made it for himself:

"Will you seek and serve Christ in all persons, loving your neighbor as yourself?"

"I will, with God's help."

The particular gift of knowing people of all ages and colors and religions and walks of life was easy to give Peter, and one that becomes a gift he can give to others. This, I think, is one of the most important things we can do for our children: teach them to draw the circle wider, help them make the world a little bit smaller. This is what the kingdom of God looks like; we are building it together and it won't be finished until everyone's in.

What Next?

I am eager for you to try some of what you've found here. Go and *do*. Your children are already in relationship with God who loves them deeply, so nurture that, help it grow, and watch what happens. Remember that you don't have to have all the answers; be willing to ask lots of questions. Trust yourself, trust that God is in this with you, find your tribe of people on the Way following Jesus and walk with them. Take risks, pray, love, serve, read, have fun!

May God bless you and keep you,
May the face of God shine upon you,
May God be gracious to you, and
May God give you peace.
Adapted from Numbers 6:24–26

A Note to Clergy and Church Educators

Christian Smith delivered the Ensign Lecture at Yale Divinity School in October 2014 and in it I heard what prompted me to write this book: the fourth wave of data from The National Study of Youth and Religion (a longitudinal study of three thousand youth) is in, and it has determined that parents are the most significant influence on the religious and spiritual lives of American teens. The study also noted that the home is where the transmittal of faith happens, that clergy and youth ministers play a very limited role in that transmission, and that ordinary life practices—not programs, or rites of passage, or preaching—are the means of transmission.

Our job is *not* to be the experts, the paid professionals. Our job is to encourage parents to accept this role as the primary pastors of their children and to give them the vocabulary they need to articulate their faith. We must reassure them that in forming their children's faith, there is room for and grace in uncertainty and doubt, questions and ambiguity. In his book, *A Generous Community*, Bishop

Andy Doyle writes, "The future Church must adopt a new way of thinking about formation. It will engage in opportunities for individuals of every age to play and experiment with Christianity and their story, as it relates to the Episcopal Way of life."[1] The future is now. We aren't in this work to impart knowledge about religion; we are in this work to share our passion about the Christian faith, to tell our story of the people of God, and to help others find their place in it. The classroom is not a model for this kind of creative, collaborative, lifelong exploration. Fortunately, we are so much more than that.

Invite your families to help shape what would be most useful to them. Use this book for a discussion group or book study, leaving time and space for practices. Take a chapter at a time, and bring in your own experiences, inviting the participants to share their own as well. Try doing this intergenerationally, so that those without children and older adults can see themselves included in "family." If we are going to talk about how we talk about God, prayer, or reading the Bible, we'll learn so much from each other.

Church is one of the few places left where we intentionally bring people of all ages together. So let's take advantage of that. After the influence of parents, research shows the biggest indicators of youth growing into an adult faith are (1) participation in worship and (2) connection to other adults in the faith community. If your church still sends children to Sunday school and teenagers to youth group during worship, it may be time to change that. Come to think of it, if your service doesn't lend itself well to the active participation of children and teens, it's probably time to change that, too.

What an exciting time this is for us! Please let me know how I can help continue the conversation.

Wendy Claire Barrie

Glossary

Baptismal Covenant. The series of vows, made by all present, in the rite of Holy Baptism. In the Episcopal Church the Baptismal Covenant is widely regarded as the normative statement of what it means to follow Christ.

Book of Common Prayer, The (BCP). The official book of worship of the Episcopal Church that provides liturgical services, prayers, and instructions about what Episcopalians believe about God, Jesus, and the Holy Spirit.

Catechism. Also called "An Outline of the Faith," this is an outline for instruction in the Christian faith presented in a question and answer format. It is found in the Book of Common Prayer.

centering prayer. A Christian contemplative practice developed in the 1970s by Trappist monks to make a medieval form of meditation accessible to modern lay people.

chorister. A person who sings in a choir.

communion of saints. The whole family of God, the living and the dead, those whom we love and those whom we hurt, bound together in Christ by sacrament, prayer, and praise.

Compline. The last of the four services of the Daily Office (BCP, 127) that is descended from the night prayers said before bed at the end of the monastic round of daily prayer.

Confirmation. The rite in which we express a mature commitment to Christ, and receive strength from the Holy Spirit through prayer and the laying on of hands by a bishop.

Examen. A formal examination of the soul or conscience through prayer; a contemplation of your own thoughts, desires, and conduct.

God. The creator of heaven and earth, of all that is, seen and unseen. The first "person" of the Trinity.

Good Shepherd. Another name for Jesus, taken from the Parable of the Good Shepherd in which the shepherd cares for his sheep so much, he would lay down his life for them.

grace. (1) God's love freely given to humanity for salvation. (2) A prayer of thanksgiving or blessing before a meal.

Jesus Christ. The Son of God, the second person of the Trinity, the savior and redeemer of humanity, the Word of God who was made flesh and dwelt among us (as human) in the world. The nature of God as revealed in Jesus is that God is love.

Holy Baptism. The sacrament by which God adopts us as children and makes us members of Christ's Body, the Church, and inheritors of the kingdom of God. The outward and visible sign in Baptism is water, in which the person is baptized in the name of the Father (God), and of the Son (Jesus), and of the Holy Spirit. The inward and spiritual grace in Baptism is union with Christ in his death and resurrection, birth into God's family in the Church, forgiveness of sins, and new life in the Holy Spirit.

Holy Bible. From the Latin *biblia* and Greek *biblios*, meaning book or books, the Bible consists of sixty-six books and letters written by more than forty authors during a period of approximately fifteen hundred years. The Old Testament (Hebrew Scriptures) are the stories of the relationship God had with his chosen people, the Hebrews. The New Testament (Christian Scriptures) are about the life of Jesus and the early Church. Also called Holy Scriptures.

Holy Eucharist. The sacrament commanded by Christ for the continual remembrance of his life, death, and resurrection, until his coming again. The outward and visible sign in the Eucharist is bread and wine. The inward and spiritual grace is the Body and Blood of Christ given to his people, and received by faith. It is also called the Lord's Supper, Holy Communion, and the Mass.

Holy Spirit. The third "person" of the Trinity; God at work in the world and in the Church even now.

labyrinth. Not a maze or puzzle to be solved, but a path of meaning to be experienced. Its path is circular and convoluted, but it does not have dead ends. A labyrinth has one entrance—one way in and one way out. Often used as a prayer practice symbolizing a journey or pilgrimage to seek God.

prayer. Responding to God, by thought and by deeds, with or without words. Jesus gave us The Lord's Prayer as an example of prayer. The principal kinds of prayer are adoration, praise, thanksgiving, penitence, oblation, intercession, and petition.

psalm. A sacred song or hymn, in particular those contained in the biblical Book of Psalms and used in Christian and Jewish worship.

resurrection. We believe that God will raise us from death in the fullness of our being, so that we may live with Christ in the communion of saints.

ritual. A religious or solemn ceremony consisting of a series of actions performed according to a prescribed order.

sabbath. (1) A day of religious observance and abstinence from work, kept by Jews from Friday evening to Saturday evening, and by most Christians on Sunday. (2) To stop, cease, or to keep rest.

sacrament. The sacraments (Holy Baptism and Holy Eucharist) are outward and visible signs of inward and spiritual grace, given by Christ as sure and certain means by which we receive that grace. Other sacramental rites that evolved in the Church under the guidance of the Holy Spirit include confirmation, ordination, holy matrimony, reconciliation of a penitent, and unction.

saint. A person acknowledged as holy or virtuous and typically regarded as being in heaven after death.

Shema. A Hebrew text consisting of three passages from the first five books of the Hebrew Scriptures (Deuteronomy 6:4, 11:13–21, Numbers 15:37–41) and beginning "Hear O Israel, the Lord our God is one Lord." It forms an important part of Jewish evening and morning prayer.

Tallis Canon. One of nine tunes written by Thomas Tallis (around 1561) that is often used in the Doxology in public worship and evening prayers. Listen here: http://cyberhymnal.org/htm/a/l/allprais.htm

Recommended Resources

For Children and Youth

Delval, Marie-Hélène. *Images of God for Young Children* (Grand Rapids: Eerdmans Books for Young Readers, 2010).

Delval, Marie-Hélène. *Psalms for Young Children* (Grand Rapids: Eerdmans Books for Young Readers, 2008).

Gamber, Jenifer C. *My Faith, My Life: Revised Edition* (New York: Morehouse Publishing, 2014).

Gamber, Jenifer C. and Sharon Ely Pearson. *Call on Me: A Prayer Book for Young People* (New York: Morehouse Publishing, 2012).

Hackenburg, Rachel. *Writing to God: Kid's Edition* (Brewster, MA: Paraclete Press, 2012).

Hanson, Warren. *The Next Place* (Minneapolis: Waldman House Press, Inc., 1997).

Hastings, Selina. *The Children's Illustrated Bible* (New York: Dorling Kindersley, 1994).

Hendrix, John. *Miracle Man: The Story of Jesus* (New York: Abrams Books, 2016).

Higgenbottham, Anastasia. *Death is Stupid (Ordinary Horrible Things)* (New York: The Feminist Press at CUNY, 2016).

Kaldor, LuAnn Schnable. *The Angels On My Tree* (Rhinebeck, NY: Four Directions Press, 2014).

Lewis, C.S. *The Lion, the Witch and the Wardrobe: The Chronicles of Narnia, Book 2* (New York: HarperCollins, 1978).

L'Engle, Madeleine. *A Wrinkle in Time Fiftieth Anniversary Commemorative Edition* (New York: Square Fish, 2012).

MacBeth, Sybil. *Praying in Color: Kid's Edition* (Brewster, MA: Paraclete Press, 2009).

McAllister, Margaret. *Women of the Bible* (Brewster, MA: Paraclete Press, 2013).

Ross, Steve. *Marked* (New York: Seabury Books, 2005).

Rylant, Cynthia. *Dog Heaven* (New York: The Blue Sky Press, 1995).

Sasso, Sandy Eisenberg. *In God's Name* (Woodstock, VT: Jewish Lights, 1994).

Shine On: A Story Bible (Elgin, IL: Brethern Press, 2014).

Spinelli, Eileen. *Somebody Loves You, Mr. Hatch* (New York: Simon & Schuster Books for Young Readers, 1991).

The CEB Student Bible (Common English Bible, 2015).

Tutu, Desmond. *Children of God Storybook Bible* (Grand Rapids: Zondervan, 2010).

Tutu, Desmond. *God's Dream* (Somerville, MA: Candlewick Press, 2008).

Viorst, Judith. *The Tenth Good Thing About Barney* (New York: Simon & Schuster, 1971).

Watts, Murray. *The Bible For Children* (Intercourse, PA: Good Books, 2002).

Wood, Douglas. *Old Turtle* (New York: Scholastic, 2007).

For Adults

Bell, Rob. *What We Talk About When We Talk About God* (New York: HarperOne, 2013).

Caldwell, Elizabeth. *I Wonder: Engaging a Child's Curiosity about the Bible* (Nashville: Abingdon Press, 2016).

Changes: Prayers and Services Honoring Rites of Passage (New York: Church Publishing, 2007).

Cox, Meg. *The Book of New Family Traditions: How to Create Great Rituals for Holidays and Every Day* (Philadelphia: Running Press Book Publishers, 2013).

David, Laurie. *The Family Dinner: Great Ways to Connect with Your Kids, One Meal at a Time* (New York: Grand Central Life & Style, 2010). http://thefamilydinnerbook. com

Dean, Kenda Creasy. *Almost Christian: What the Faith of Our Teenagers Is Telling the American Church* (New York: Oxford University Press, 2010).

Given, Emily Slichter. *Building Faith Brick by Brick: An Imaginative Way to Explore the Bible with Children* (Denver: Morehouse Education Resources, 2014).

Grollman, Earl A. *Talking About Death: A Dialogue Between Parent and Child* (Boston: Beacon Press, 1990).

Hackenburg, Rachel. *Writing to God: 40 Days of Praying with My Pen* (Brewster, MA: Paraclete Press, 2011).

Hutchison, Roger. *The Painting Table: A Journal of Loss and Joy* (New York: Morehouse Publishing, 2013).

Kushner, Harold. *When Bad Things Happen to Good People* (New York: Random House, 1981).

Lamott, Anne. *Help, Thanks, Wow: The Three Essential Prayers* (New York: Penguin Group, 2012).

L'Engle, Madeleine. *A Stone for a Pillow* (Wheaton, IL: Harold Shaw Publishers, 1986).

MacBeth, Sybil. *Praying in Color: Drawing a New Path to God* (Brewster, MA: Paraclete Press, 2007).

Miller, Lisa. *The Spiritual Child: The New Science on Parenting for Health and Lifelong Thriving* (New York: St. Martin's Press, 2015).

Peterson, Eugene. *The Message: The Bible in Contemporary Language* (Colorado Springs: NavPress, 2007).

Pritchard, Gretchen Wolff. *Offering the Gospel to Children* (Boston: Cowley Publications, 1992).

Websites and Online Resources

Building Faith *www.buildfaith.org*
Resources and ideas from across the Episcopal Church curated by a team at Virginia Theological Seminary.

Candle Press *www.candlepress.com*
Note especially the "To Go" section intended for families with young children as well as the resources for Holy Baptism and Holy Eucharist.

Emily Scott, pastor of St. Lydia's in Brooklyn, gave a powerful speech to 30,000 Lutheran teenagers and all the bishops of the Evangelical Lutheran Church in America in July 2015. You can watch it here: *https://www.youtube.com/watch?v=ixuw2JwVsB4*

Grow Christians *www.growchristians.org*
An online community for parents sponsored by Forward Movement and Plainsong Farm.

Illustrated Children's Ministry *www.illustratedchildrens ministry.com/families/*
Really cool illustrated coloring pages and posters as well as seasonal devotions and activities for families.

Meditation for Christians *philfoxrose.com/meditation-for-christians.*
"Meditation for Christians" is Phil Fox Rose's introduction to a Christian practice of meditation.

Milestones Ministry *https://store.milestonesministry.org/*
The source for blessing bowls and stones; also look for their "Faith Talk" cards to use at home.

Momastery *www.momastery.com*
Glennon Doyle Melton's online community of "truth-tellers and hope-spreaders;" think "monastery," but for mothers and others.

My Faith, My Life *www.myfaithmylife.org*
Resources geared toward Episcopal youth ages 12–18 from Jenifer Gamber.

Sleepytime Club *www.sleepytimeclub.com*
Mom, musician, author, and educator Brook Packard offers ways and tunes for helping create meaningful memories at bedtime for you and your children.

The Bible Project *www.jointhebibleproject.com*
Timothy Mackie and Jonathan Collins began this crowd-funded nonprofit video project in 2014 with the intent of changing how people read and use the Bible.

Traci Smith *www.etsy.com/shop/AuthorTraciSmith*
Pastor Traci Smith has printable resources for families, including a "family faith jar" with conversation starters, prayers, and practices that can be done in five to ten minutes.

Who Are You Jesus? *http://whoareyoujesus.com/*
A new and beautiful app for children that invites them
to creatively engage with scripture.

Wendy Claire Barrie *https://wendyclairebarrie.com*
This is my blog, where you'll find further writing exploring faith at home as well as resources and links to Pinterest, other writers and websites.

Acknowledgments

Everything I do well, I do in collaboration with others.

I am deeply grateful for the encouragement, guidance and skill of my editor, Sharon Ely Pearson. Without her mentorship over the last fifteen years, I would not have pursued Christian formation as my profession, let alone written a book about it.

I have been formed in several remarkable communities of faith, most notably:
> St. Mary's Episcopal Church, Laguna Beach, California
> St. Margaret of Scotland Episcopal Church and School,
>   San Juan Capistrano, California
> Church of the Epiphany, New York City
> All Saints Church, Pasadena, California
> St. Lydia's Church, Brooklyn, New York

So many people in so many categories have made significant contributions "in thought, word and deed" to what has ended up within these pages. Special thanks go to:

Some of the wonderful clergy who have nurtured me: Bradford Karelius, Myron Bloy, Andrew Mullins, Margaret

Peckham Clark, Ed Bacon, Shannon Ferguson Kelly, Wilma Jakobsen, Pamela Strobel, Edward Sunderland, Emily Scott and Rabbi Mitchell Hurvitz.

The outstanding faculty of the Forma Certificate Program in Leadership of Lifelong Christian Formation: Lisa Kimball (who also came up with this book's snappy subtitle), Julie Lytle, Victoria Garvey, and Donald Schell, and those in its first cohort: Katherine Kanto Doyle, Kate McKey-Dunar, Charlotte Hand Greeson, Anne Karoly, and Polly Gurley Redd.

Dear friends whose faith, friendship and stories have fed and enlightened me: Margo Clarke, Linda Kilpatrick, Janna Wright, Susan Remsberg and Anna Remsberg Marquez, Linda Clapp, Brad and Sue Bremer, Kathy Manganiello, Melissa Wallace, Helen Angove and Matthew Graham, Holly Evans, Jann Lacoss and Kathy Johnson, Jennifer Cowie King, Mary Jane Parks, MaryAlice Raabe, Jenifer Gamber, Missy Morain, Cathy Ode, Day Smith Pritchartt, Karla Thomas, Leslie Jeffries, Kathy McKenzie and Greg Pitkoff, Wendalyn Nichols, Yana Wagg and Chris Gardephe, Sensho Wagg, and Carrie Youngberg.

My wonderful, supportive colleagues at Trinity Wall Street and the families of the 9:15 service at St. Paul's Chapel in New York City.

Finally, much love and thanks to my parents, Deborah and Michael and my siblings Gregg and Amy for their encouragement, and to my son Peter Philip and my husband Phil Fox Rose, for, well, *everything*.

Notes

Introduction

1. These thoughts were planted in me after reading Diana Butler Bass's *Christianity after Religion: The End of Church and the Birth of a New Spiritual Awakening* (New York: Harper Collins), 116–20.

2. Bass, 149.

3. From the Right Reverend Michael Curry's sermon from the 77th General Convention of The Episcopal Church in Indianapolis, Indiana, on July 7, 2012.

4. https://theamericanscholar.org/i-will-love-you-in-the-summertime/#.V2o6JMrLeR

Chapter 1

1. 1 Kings 19:12.

2. www.ucc.org/god-is-still-speaking (accessed May 30, 2016).

3. Christian Smith with Melinda Lundquist Denton, *Soul Searching: The Religious and Spiritual Lives of American Teenagers* (New York: Oxford University Press), 164–65.

4. Acts 17:28.

5. Smith, 131.

6. Smith, 133.

7. Elizabeth Johnson, *Quest for the Living God: Mapping Frontiers in the Theology of God* (New York: Bloomsbury Academic, 2007), 17–19.

8. Johnson, 15.

9. www.uscatholic.org/church/2008/06/honor-your-father-and-your-mother (accessed June 1, 2016).

10. Rob Bell, *What We Talk About When We Talk About God* (New York: HarperOne, 2013), 131–2.

Chapter 2

1. Søren Kierkegaard, (1813–1855).

2. Anne Lamott, *Help, Thanks, Wow: The Three Essential Prayers* (New York: Penguin Group, 2012), 1.

3. The Book of Common Prayer (BCP), 856.

4. http://greatergood.berkeley.edu/expandinggratitude

5. Jenifer C. Gamber and Sharon Ely Pearson, *Call on Me: A Prayer Book for Young People* (New York: Morehouse Publishing, 2012), 60. Used with permission.

6. BCP, 134.

7. The Anglican Church in Aotearoa, New Zealand and Polynesia. *A New Zealand Prayer Book* (San Francisco: HarperCollins, 1989), 184.

Chapter 3

1. Madeleine L'Engle. *A Stone for a Pillow* (Wheaton, IL: Harold Shaw Publishers, 1986), 80.

2. Fredrica Harris Thompsett, *We Are Theologians: Strengthening the People of God* (New York: Church Publishing, 2004), 70.

3. Jennifer Bird, *Permission Granted: Take the Bible into Your Own Hands* (Louisville: Westminster John Knox Press, 2015),

4. Bird, 189.

5. *The Children's Adventure Bible* (Grand Rapids, MI: Zonderkidz, 2013), 1399.

6. *Children's Adventure Bible*, 1400.

7. Sally Lloyd-Jones. *The Jesus Storybook Bible* (Grand Rapids: Zondervan, 2007).

8. www.godlyplay.org

9. http://www.tcd.ie/Library/bookofkells/ (accessed April 14, 2016).

10. Elizabeth W Corrie, editor. *The CEB Student Bible* (Nashville: Common English Bible, 2015), xv.

11. https://jointhebibleproject.com/our-story/

12. http://stlydias.org

13. Mark 3:21.

14. Mark 16:8.

Chapter 4

1. Acts 2:44–47.

2. Bass, 149.

3. Galatians 3:28.

4. http://www.intergenerationalfaith.com/uploads/5/1/6/4/5164069/the_church_sticking_together.pdf, 19.

5. Gretchen Wolff Pritchard, *Offering the Gospel to Children* (Boston: Cowley Publications, 1992), 65.

6. Pritchard, 68.

7. You can find more ideas at Sharon Pearson's blog, *Rows of Sharon*: https://rowsofsharon.com/2016/04/07/a-childs-worship-bag/ (accessed May 23, 2016).

8. BCP, 857.

9. BCP, 298.

10. Matthew 3:17.

11. Helen Barron, *Journey Into Baptism* (Denver: Candle Press, 2016), 5.

12. The service of Holy Baptism can be found in The Book of Common Prayer, beginning on page 299.

13. Barron, 21.

14. Holy Eucharist, Rite II begins on page 355 of The Book of Common Prayer.

15. Pritchard, 162.

16. Rainer Maria Rilke, *Letters to a Young Poet* (New York: Random House, 1984), Stephen Mitchell translation, 34.

17. John H. Westerhoff, *A People Called Episcopalians, revised edition* (New York: Church Publishing, 2015), 35.

18. BCP, 308.

Chapter 5

1. www.thekingcenter.org/about-dr-king and www.
archives.gov/press/exhibits/dream-speech.pdf (accessed
May 30, 2016).
2. BCP, 265 and Genesis 3:19.
3. BCP, 308.
4. John 13:35.
5. John 1:5.
6. www.patheos.com/blogs/philfoxrose/2013/03/the-
not-so-christian-roots-of-hot-cross-buns-with-a-recipe/
(accessed May 26, 2016).
7. www.youtube.com/watch?v=qtfAQiW9xPQ
8. http://prayer.forwardmovement.org/the_calendar.
php?k=3

Chapter 6

1. Laurie David, *The Family Dinner: Great Ways to
Connect with Your Kids, One Meal at a Time* (New York:
Grand Central Life & Style, 2010), 200.
2. Christine King Farris, *My Brother Martin: A Sister
Remembers Growing Up with the Rev. Dr. Martin Luther
King Jr.* (New York: Simon & Schuster, 2003), 30.
3. www.nytimes.com/2013/03/17/fashion/the-family-
stories-that-bind-us-this-life.html?_r=0
4. www.theatlantic.com/education/archive/2013/12/
what-kids-learn-from-hearing-family-stories/282075/
5. During her talk given at "Why Christian?" a confer-
ence held in Minneapolis, Minnesota, September 18–20,
2015.

6. "Why Christian?" 2015.

7. BCP, 830.

8. Aran Walter, "Film School, for Sunday School," *Building Faith*, April 8, 2016, www.buildfaith.org/2016/04/08/film-school-not-sunday-school/ (accessed April 27 2016).

9. www.npr.org/2011/06/18/137223191/father-daughter-reading-streak-lasts-nearly-9-years (accessed May 26, 2016).

10. www.nytimes.com/2010/03/21/fashion/21GenB.html?_r=0 (accessed May 26, 2016).

11. www.sleepytimeclub.com/344-2/ (accessed May 26, 2016).

12. Brook Packard, "Flowing Stream" from *Heart Bedtime Kit*, www.sleepytimeclub.com/sleepytime-store/. Used with permission.

13. Meg Cox, *The Book of New Family Traditions: How to Create Great Rituals for Holidays and Every Day* (Philadelphia: Running Press Book Publishers, 2013), 172.

14. http://thepioneerwoman.com/entertainment/the-five-things-i-learned-from-george-bailey/

15. www.kingofpeace.org/resources/petfuneralliturgy.htm

16. Cox, 14.

17. http://store.milestonesministry.org/product-p/mbbm.htm

18. Cesare Pavese, *The Business of Living: Diaries 1935–1950* (New Brunswick, NJ: Transaction Publishers, 2009), 172

Chapter 7

1. Harold S. Kushner, *When Bad Things Happen to Good People* (New York: Anchor Books, 1981), 154.

2. www.fredrogers.org/parents/special-challenges/tragic-events.php#sthash.dkbuzkns.dpuf (accessed May 27, 2016).

3. Melissa Florer-Bixler, "Children at the Grave: Making Space for Grief," *The Christian Century* Vol. 133, No. 6 (March 4, 2016).

4. Frederick Buechner, *Beyond Words: Daily Readings in the ABC's of Faith* (San Francisco: Harper Collins, 2004), 139.

Chapter 8

1. Emily Scott at the National Youth Gathering of the ELCA held in Detroit's Ford Field stadium on August 2, 2015.

2. http://www.crossroadsnyc.org

3. http://mcc.gse.harvard.edu/files/gse-mcc/files/mcc-research-report.pdf?m=1448057487

4. http://mcc.gse.harvard.edu/parenting-resources-raising-caring-ethical-children/cultivating-empathy

5. http://momastery.com/blog/2011/08/28/dear-chase-2/ (emphasis in original)

6. Deuteronomy 6:4–9.

A Note to Clergy and Church Educators

1. C. Andrew Doyle, *A Generous Community: Being the Church in a New Missionary Age* (New York: Morehouse, 2016), 141.